GOLDEN WORDS UPON GOLDEN WORDS...FOR EVERY MUSLIM.

"Imaam al-Barbahaaree, may Allaah have mercy upon him said:

May Allaah have mercy upon you! Examine carefully the speech of everyone you hear from in your time particularly. So do not act in haste and do not enter into anything from it until you ask and see: Did any of the Companions of the Prophet, may Allaah's praise and salutations be upon him, speak about it, or did any of the scholars? So if you find a narration from them about it, cling to it, do not go beyond it for anything and do not give precedence to anything over it and thus fall into the Fire.

Explanation by Sheikh Saaleh al-Fauzaan, may Allaah preserve him:

'Do not be hasty in accepting as correct what you may hear from the people especially in these later times. As now there are many who speak about so many various matters, issuing rulings and ascribing to themselves both knowledge and the right to speak. This is especially the case after the emergence and spread of new modern day media technologies. Such that everyone now can speak and bring forth that which is in truth worthless; by this meaning words of no true value - speaking about whatever they wish in the name of knowledge and in the name of the religion of Islaam. It has even reached the point that you find the people of misguidance and the members of the various groups of misguidance and deviance from the religion speaking as well. Such individuals have now become those who speak in the name of the religion of Islaam through means such as the various satellite television channels. Therefore be very cautious!

It is upon you oh Muslim, and upon you oh student of knowledge individually, to verify matters and not rush to embrace everything and anything you may hear. It is upon you to verify the truth of what you hear, asking, 'Who else also makes this same statement or claim?', 'Where did this thought or concept originate or come from?', 'Who is its reference or source authority?'. Asking what are the evidences which support it from within the Book and the Sunnah? And inquiring where has the individual who is putting this forth studied and taken his knowledge from? From who has he studied the knowledge of Islaam?

Each of these matters requires verification through inquiry and investigation, especially in the present age and time. As it is not every speaker who should rightly be considered a source of knowledge, even if he is well spoken and eloquent, and can manipulate words captivating his listeners. Do not be taken in and accept him until you are aware of the degree and scope of what he possesses of knowledge and understanding. As perhaps someone's words may be few, but possess true understanding, and perhaps another will have a great deal of speech yet he is actually ignorant to such a degree that he doesn't actually posses anything of true understanding. Rather he only has the ability to enchant with his speech so that the people are deceived. Yet he puts forth the perception that he is a scholar, that he is someone of true understanding and comprehension, that he is a capable thinker, and so forth. Through such means and ways he is able to deceive and beguile the people, taking them away from the way of truth.

Therefore what is to be given true consideration is not the amount of the speech put forth or that one can extensively discuss a subject. Rather the criterion that is to be given consideration is what that speech contains within it of sound authentic knowledge, what it contains of the established and transmitted principles of Islaam. As perhaps a short or brief statement which is connected to or has a foundation in the established principles can be of greater benefit than a great deal of speech which simply rambles on, and through hearing you don't actually receive very much benefit from.

This is the reality which is present in our time; one sees a tremendous amount of speech which only possesses within it a small amount of actual knowledge. We see the presence of many speakers yet few people of true understanding and comprehension.' "

[The eminent major scholar Sheikh Saaleh al-Fauzaan, may Allaah preserve him- 'A Valued Gift for the Reader Of Comments Upon the Book Sharh as-Sunnah', page 102-103]

This pocket edition is a selection taken from the larger book:

Statements of the Guiding Scholars of Our Age Regarding Books & their Advice to the Beginner Seeker of Knowledge

With Selections from the Following Scholars:
Sheikh 'Abdul-'Azeez ibn 'Abdullah ibn Baaz -Sheikh Muhammad ibn Saaleh al-'Utheimein - Sheikh Muhammad Naasiruddeen al-Albaanee - Sheikh Muqbil ibn Haadee al-Waada'ee - Sheikh 'Abdur-Rahman ibn Naaser as-Sa'adee - Sheikh Muhammad 'Amaan al-Jaamee - Sheikh Muhammad al-Ameen as-Shanqeetee - Sheikh Ahmad ibn Yahya an-Najmee
(May Allaah have mercy upon them.) &
Sheikh Saaleh al-Fauzaan ibn 'Abdullah al-Fauzaan - Sheikh Saaleh ibn 'Abdul-'Azeez Aal-Sheikh - Sheikh Muhammad ibn 'Abdul-Wahhab al-Wasaabee -Permanent Committee to Scholastic Research & Issuing Of Islamic Rulings
(May Allaah preserve them.)

With an introduction by:
Sheikh Muhammad Ibn 'Abdullah al-Imaam
Collected and Translated
by Abu Sukhailah Khalil Ibn-Abelahyi al-Amreekee

[Available: **Now**¦ pages: **370+**
price: (Soft cover) **$25**
(Hard cover) **$32**
(eBook) **$9.99**]

A TREASURY OF GUIDANCE FOR THE MUSLIM STRIVING TO LEARN HIS RELIGION:
SHEIKH 'ABDUL-'AZEEZ IBN 'ABDULLAH IBN BAAZ

Statements of the Guiding Scholars Pocket Edition 5

Translated & Compiled By
Abu Sukhailah Khalil Ibn-Abelahyi al-Amreekee

Table of Contents

Images of handwritten original introduction of Sheikh Muhammad Ibn 'Abdullah al-Imaam (may Allaah preserve him)

بسم الله الرحمن الرحيم

دار الحديث للعلوم الشرعية
محمد بن عبدالله الإمام

التاريخ ١٨ / ٧ / ١٤٢٥هـ

الحمد لله والصلاة والسلام على رسول الله وعلى آله وصحبه

أما بعد

لقد اطلعت على الأخ / خليل بن إبراهيم حفظه الله
على ما به من أنه يجمع كلام بعض أهل العلم في الكتب
التي ينصح المسلمون بقراءتها والكتب التي يحذر المسلمون
من قراءتها فرأيته قد جمع جمعا طيبا مما هو من هذا العلم
فأسأل الله المسؤول أن ينفع بذلك وهذا من فضل الله
على أخينا الغالي ظهور المذكور رأيت أن يكون والله على
الخير مقتديا بالرسول صلى الله عليه وسلم في ذلك الذي قال فيه عليه
الصلاة والسلام « إنما على الأرض خير» فلهذا أقول خيرا على

اليمن – لواء ذمار – معبر – هاتف : ٤٣٠٥٢١ – تلفاكس : ٤٣٠٢٨٠ – ص . ب : ٨٦٠٠١

12

Images of handwritten original introduction of Sheikh Muhammad Ibn 'Abdullah al-Imaam (may Allaah preserve him)

INTRODUCTION OF
SHEIKH MUHAMMAD IBN 'ABDULLAH AL-IMAAM
(MAY ALLAAH PRESERVE HIM)

All praise is due to Allaah, may Allaah's praise and His salutations be upon the Messenger of Allaah, his family, and Companions.

As for what follows:

The brother Khalil Ibn-Abelahyi, may Allaah preserve him, has shown to me that which he has undertaken in gathering the speech of some of the people of knowledge regarding the books the Muslims are advised to read, as well as those books that the Muslims are warned against reading.

After reading it, I see that he has compiled a collection from the statements of well-known people of knowledge, and he has selected well and brought forth good for the Muslims in what he presents to them in this blessed book. How can this not be so, when the foundation of every good is in reading the book that possesses benefit and in having a righteous teacher? As the scholars have mentioned, *"The one who carefully selects his teacher and his book has protected his religion with the best of safeguards."*

Sheikh Ibn al-'Utheimeen, may Allaah have mercy upon him, was asked, "At whose hands should we take knowledge?" He replied, *"From the one of correct beliefs, sound methodology, and the proper goal and objective."* Likewise, the author of the 'Risaa'il al-Islaah' stated,

"*The rectification of the Muslim nation is through the correction of its deeds and endeavors, and the correction of its deeds and endeavors is based upon the rectification of its branches of knowledge, and the rectification of its branches of knowledge lies in the reliable transmitters of its knowledge.*" Consider what Ibn Taymeeyah has said regarding Abee Haamed al-Ghazaalee: "*The book ash-Shifaa' caused him to become afflicted...*" (Majmu'a al-Fatawaa, Vol. 10, Page 552). Meaning that the illness of Abu Haamed originated from the reading and studying the book ash-Shifaa' of Ibn Sinaa, due to what it contains of deviations that lead one outside of Islaam. May Allaah be generous to the one who said:

We ceased our brotherhood with those
>   *who became diseased from the Book Ash-Shifaa'*
And how many times have I said, oh people you are
>   *on the very edge of the cliff because of the book*
>   *Ash- Shifaa' '*
When they dismissed our warning to them
>   *we return in death, back to Allaah with Him being*
>   *sufficient for us,*
Yet they then died upon the religion of Ibn Rustaalas!
>   *while we lived upon the way of the chosen Messenger.*

(Majmu'a al-Fatawaa, Vol. 9, Page 253)

Therefore from the completeness of a Muslim's protection from harm and trials is that he does not acquire a book or choose it for reading or study until he inquires about that book from someone whom he knows is reliable in both his religion and his knowledge.

How many diseases of our Muslim nation are caused by reading books that are not truly reliable when judging according to the guidance of the Sharee'ah! Therefore as a statement of ample warning regarding every book in which its harm is known to be greater than its good, it is not permissible to publish it, read it, or give it as a gift.

As for the books of the sects of the Raafidhah, the Sufeeyah, the people of philosophical argument and false rhetoric- then it should be known assuredly that their evil and harm is significantly greater than any good within them. So from the completeness of a Muslim's protecting himself from harm and trials is that he does not acquire a book or choose it for reading or study until he inquires about that book from someone whom he knows is reliable regarding his religion and knowledge.

Written by
Muhammad Ibn 'Abdullah al-Imaam

COMPILER'S INTRODUCTION
(POCKET EDITION)

In the name of Allaah, The Most Gracious, The Most Merciful

Verily, all praise is due to Allaah, we praise Him, we seek His assistance and we ask for His forgiveness. We seek refuge in Him from the evils of our souls and the evils of our actions. Whoever Allaah guides, no one can lead him astray and whoever is caused to go astray, there is no one that can guide him. I bear witness that there is no deity worthy of worship except Allaah alone with no partners. And I bear witness that Muhammad is His worshipper and Messenger.

Oh you who believe, fear Allaah as He ought to be feared and do not die except while you are Muslims. -(Surah Aal-'Imraan:102)

Oh mankind, fear Allaah who created you from a single soul and from that, He created its mate. And from them He brought forth many men and women. And fear Allaah to whom you demand your mutual rights. Verily, Allaah is an ever All-Watcher over you. -(Surah an-Nisaa:1)

Oh you who believe, fear Allaah and speak a word that is truthful (and to the point) - He will rectify your deeds and forgive you your sins. And whoever obeys Allaah and His Messenger has achieved a great success. -(Surah al-Ahzaab:70-71)

As for what follows:

The best speech is the book of Allaah, and the best guidance is the guidance of Muhammad, may Allaah's praise and His salutations be upon him. And the worst of affairs are newly invented matters in the religion, and every newly invented matter in an innovation, and every innovation is a going astray, and every going astray is in the Fire.

Certainly, every Muslim hopes for success and happiness in this world and the Hereafter. Our Lord has taught us to ask Him for guidance in the "Mother" of al-Qur'aan, Surah al-Faatihah, where He explains to us exactly which path is the true path to contentment and the true way of success. The guiding scholar Sheikh 'Abdul-'Azeez Ibn 'Abdullah Ibn Baaz, may Allaah have mercy upon him, comprehensively described this path to happiness:

*"...the path to happiness and the path to success is the path which was taken by the first believers, the Companions of the Prophet, may Allaah's praise and His salutations be upon him, and those who followed them in goodness. As Allaah, the Majestic and the Exalted, says, ❁ ... **this is my straight path. Follow it and do not follow the other paths as they will separate you from His path. This is what he has ordained for you, in order that you may become righteous.** ❁ –(Surah al-Anaam: 153) The path of Allaah is knowledge, this truly is His path, this truly is guidance, this truly is Islaam, this truly is goodness, and this truly is the fear of Allaah.*

*Regarding this, Allaah, Glorified and Exalted, says in Surah al-Faatihah, ❁**Guide us to the straight path.**❁ Our Lord has instructed us to ask for this; instructed that we ask from Him guidance to His straight path. And His straight path is that knowledge that was brought by His Messenger, as well as acting according to that."* [1]

The hadeeth scholar Sheikh Hamaad Ibn al-Ansaaree, may Allaah have mercy upon him, explained the meaning this verse, ❁ *Guide us to the straight path* ❁ which is recited by all of us in our ritual prayers:

---

[1]   From our sheikh's comments upon "Understanding of the Religion' by Sheikh Saaleh al-Fauzaan

"The meaning of ﴾ **Guide us to the straight path** ﴿ *is: Our Lord whom we have praised by means of what You have taught us. We ask You and supplicate to You by this supplication, which You have taught us, that You guide us to the straight path. And the meaning of* ﴾ **Guide us to the straight path** ﴿ *is: Teach us that which will benefit us, and then grant us success to act in accordance with that which benefits us.'"* [2]

Indeed, from the greatest means to achieving this foundation of success and happiness; is the seeking of beneficial knowledge and acting according to it. As was mentioned by Sheikh al-Islaam Ibn Taymeeyah, may Allaah have mercy upon him:

"The seeking of Sharee'ah knowledge is generally a communal obligation upon the Muslims together collectively, except for that which has been specified as an obligation for each and every individual. For example, the seeking of knowledge of what Allaah has commanded everyone in general and what He has forbidden for them. The obtainment of that type of knowledge is considered an obligation upon every individual. As it has been narrated in the two 'Saheeh' collections from the Prophet, may Allaah's praise and His salutations be upon him, that he said, {The one whom Allaah intends good for He gives him understanding of his religion.}" [3] [4]

---

[2]   Risaa'il feel-Aqeedah: page 22

[3]   This hadeeth {*The one whom Allaah intends…*} is found in Saheeh al-Bukhaaree: 71, 3116, 7312/ Saheeh Muslim: 1037/ Sunan Ibn Maajah: 221/ al-Muwatta Maalik: 1300, 1667/ Musnad Imaam Ahmad: 16395, 16404, and other narrations/ Musannaf Ibn Abee Shaaybah: 31792/ & Sunan ad-Daramee: 224, 226/- on the authority of Mu'aweeyah. And it is found in Jaame' al-Tirmidhee: 2645/ Musnad Imaam Ahmad: 2786/ & Sunan ad-Daaramee: 270, 2706/- on the authority of Ibn Abbaas. And it is found in Sunan Ibn Maajah: 220/ & Musannaf 'Abdul-Razzaaq: 30851/- on the authority of Abee Hurairah. It was declared authentic by Sheikh al-Albanee in Saheeh al-Aadab al-Mufrad: 517, Silsilat al-Hadeeth as-Saheehah: 1194, 1195, 1196, Saheeh at-Targheeb at-Tarheeb: 67, as well as in other of his books. Sheikh Muqbil declared it authentic in al-Jaame' al-Saheeh: 9, 3123, 4650, may Allaah have mercy upon them both

[4]   Majmu'a al-Fatawaa: vol. 28/80

The guiding scholar Sheikh Ibn Baaz, may Allaah have mercy upon him, explained the meaning of "Sharee'ah" knowledge:

"Knowledge is known to possess many merits. Certainly the noblest field of knowledge which the seekers can strive towards, and those who aspire can endeavor to reach, is gaining Sharee'ah knowledge. While the term 'knowledge' is used generally to refer to many things, within the statements of the scholars of Islaam what is intended by 'knowledge' is Sharee'ah knowledge. This is the meaning of knowledge in its general usage as expressed in the Book of Allaah and in the texts of the Sunnah of His Messenger, may Allaah's praise and His salutations be upon him. This is knowledge of Allaah and His names and attributes, knowledge of His right over those He created, and of what commands He legislated for them, Glorified and Exalted is He. It is knowledge of the true way and path, that which leads and directs toward Him, as well as its specific details. It is knowledge of the final state and destination in the next life of all those beings He created. This is Sharee'ah knowledge, and it is the highest type of knowledge. It is worthy of being sought after and its achievement should be aspired to.

Through this knowledge one understands who Allaah, Glorified and Exalted, is, and by means of it you are able to worship Him. Through this knowledge you understand what Allaah has permitted and what He has prohibited, what He is pleased with and what He is displeased with. And through this knowledge you understand the destiny of this life and its inevitable conclusion. That being that a group of the people will end in Paradise, achieving happiness, and the rest of the people, who are indeed the majority, will end in Hellfire, the abode of disgrace and misery." [5]

---

[5]   From a lecture given by the eminent scholar at the Islamic University in Medinah on 3/26/1404

Therefore, it becomes clear that this desired goal which leads to true success, as has been mentioned, is only possible through the seeking of beneficial knowledge, meaning Sharee'ah knowledge, from its carriers- the scholars. Similarly, what is meant by the term 'scholars' are those people of knowledge from the saved and victorious group of Muslims who have always remained upon the guidance of the Messenger, may Allaah's praise and His salutations be upon him and his Companions, inwardly and outwardly, in every generation and age. They are the people of true guidance, the well-grounded scholars of Ahlus-Sunnah wa al-Jama'ah from the early generations, the later generations, and our present day scholars.

We must recognize them and affirm their position, defend their honor, and strive to assist and cooperate with them because they carry and preserve the inheritance of the Messenger of Allaah, may Allaah's praise and salutations be upon him. Sheikh al-Islaam Ibn Taymeeyah mentioned in his book, '*Lifting the Blame*', Page 10:

"It is obligatory upon the Muslims after loyalty to Allaah the Exalted and His Messenger, to have loyalty to the believers, as is mentioned in the Qur'aan. This is especially true in regard to the scholars, as they are the inheritors of the prophets and are those who have been placed in a position by Allaah like the stars by which we are guided through the darkness of land and sea.

The Muslims are in consensus regarding their guidance and knowledge. Since in every nation before the sending of our Prophet Muhammad, may Allaah's praise and His salutations be upon him, their scholars were indeed the worst of their people, until the time of the Muslim Ummah; as certainly the scholars of the Muslims are the best of them. They are the successors of the Messenger, may Allaah's praise and His salutations be upon him, in his nation, and they give life to that which has died from his Sunnah…"

It is necessary that every Muslim understand the importance of the role of the scholars and their position in our lives, being connected to them, and listening to their advice and guidance. Thereafter, it is upon us to maintain as strong connection and relationship to them as possible. Additionally, it is necessary for us to be aware of the deception, delusions, and falsehoods of those who strive to separate or distance the Muslims from our scholars, specifically coming from those people of division and group partisanship who falsely accuse the scholars of not understanding the current situation of the world, among their other false claims. They are the ones who fail to give the scholars their proper position among the people nor acknowledge their rights upon the people. The guiding scholar Saaleh al-Fauzaan, may Allaah preserve him, stated in his book, '*The Obligation of Confirming Affairs and Honoring the Scholars and an Explanation of their Position in this Ummah*' (Page 45):

"Specifically, we hear this in our time and age from those who speak attacking their honor and who falsely accuse the scholars of ignorance, short-sightedness and a lack of understanding of current affairs, as they claim; and this is a very dangerous matter. Because if we are deprived of the reliable ones from the Muslim scholars, who will lead the Muslim Ummah? Who will be turned to for rulings and judgments?

And I believe this to be a devised plan from our enemies. This is a plan which has deceived many who do not properly understand matters and those who do possess an intense love and strong enthusiasm for Islaam, but which is only based upon ignorance. So they have intense love and strong enthusiasm for Islaam, but the matter is not that simple. Since the most highly honored position in this Ummah is that of the scholars. It is not permitted to disparage them or accuse them of ignorance and short-sightedness, or with seeking the pleasure of the rulers or to describe them as the 'scholars of the rulers' or other such descriptions. This is extremely dangerous, oh worshiper of Allaah! So let us fear Allaah in regard to this matter and take caution. Clearly, it is as the poet said,

Oh scholars of the religion, oh 'salt' of the land,

What will rectify our affair, if the 'salt' itself is corrupt?'

Therefore this connection and relationship between the Muslim and the scholar is a necessity for every Muslim and especially for the beginning student of knowledge. The esteemed major scholar Sheikh Muqbil Ibn Haadee al-Waadiee, may Allaah have mercy on him, stated in '*Tuhfat al-Mujeeb 'alaa Asilaat al-Hadhar wa Ghareeb*' (Page 181-182):

"...So the cure is in returning to the Book of Allaah and the Sunnah of the Messenger of Allaah, may Allaah's praise and His salutations be upon him and his household, and then by returning to the scholars. As Allaah says, ❦ **And when there came to them a matter concerning (public) security or fear, they announced it to the people. But if only they had referred it back to the Messenger or to those charged with authority amongst them, those who have the ability to derive a proper conclusion from it would have understood it.** ❦ *-(Surah an-Nisaa:83) Therefore it is an obligation upon us to turn to the scholars in our affairs:* ❦ **These are the parables that We send forth to the people, yet no one (truly) understands them except those with knowledge.'** ❦ *-(Surah al-'Ankaboot: 43)*

But what you see is some of the people merely memorizing three or four subjects and then taking that to the masjids, thrusting themselves forward and confronting others. Then his companions designate him 'Sheikh al-Islaam'! Is this to be considered knowledge?!?

Rather, the matter of knowledge is sitting upon a mat with your legs beneath you, being patient with the necessary hunger and poverty that comes with seeking knowledge. Consider the state of the Companions of the Messenger of Allaah, may Allaah's praise and His salutations be upon him and his household, and what they were patient in the face of.

In addition, the people of knowledge- they are the ones who put matters in their proper places, as established in the previous noble verse where Allaah, the One free from imperfection and Exalted says,❮ Verily, in that is a reminder to those who possess knowledge. ❯-(Surah ar-Room: 22)'"

In summarizing what has been mentioned of the importance of this relationship between the worshippers of Allaah and the guiding scholars, the major scholar Sheikh al-Fauzaan, may Allaah preserve him, said in his book, *'Explanation of the Mistakes of Some Authors'* (Page 18):

"Oh Muslim youth! Oh students of knowledge! Connect yourselves to your scholars, attach yourselves to them, and take knowledge from them. Attach yourselves to the reliable scholars well known for the correctness of their beliefs and the soundness of their methodology, in order that you may take knowledge from them and establish your connection with your Prophet, may Allaah's praise and His salutations be upon him, as your pious predecessors did. The Muslims have never ceased receiving this knowledge from their Prophet, through their scholars, generation after every generation."

And if one were to ask: "Who are the reliable well-known scholars?' meaning by this those well grounded in knowledge? Imaam Ibn-Qayyim, may Allaah have mercy upon him, stated:

"The one who is well grounded in knowledge; if he is confronted with uncertain matters as numerous as the waves of the ocean, his certainty and steadfastness is not affected nor diminished, nor is he afflicted by doubt. As he is steadfast and well grounded in his knowledge, he is not disturbed by such uncertainties and doubts. Rather, what occurs with one such as this is in fact the repulsion of doubts due to his being safeguarded by his knowledge and the disturbances are thus bound and subdued...." [6]

Certainly, Allaah facilitated for me the compilation of some of the statements of advice from the scholars regarding seeking knowledge and beneficial books, as well as their warnings against books containing misguidance. Initially, this was simply to remove ignorance from myself and the members of my family, and then afterwards also for my brothers and sisters who are also seeking knowledge. This is in order that we all are able to strive to proceed with correct methods and manners in our seeking of beneficial knowledge. This was accomplished only with the assistance of Allaah, the Most Generous.

I ask Allaah the Majestic to make this effort purely for His sake, and to accept it from me. I hope that this will be a beneficial book in this subject and area, for the one who seeks adherence to the religion of truth through the learning of beneficial knowledge -wherever they may be in the world. As was mentioned by Sheikh al-Islaam Ibn Taymeeyah, may Allaah the Exalted have mercy upon him, understanding the nature and source of beneficial knowledge is essential to obtaining it:

"...As for which books can be utilized and relied upon in the various areas of knowledge, then this is an extensive matter. Additionally, this differs according to the differences among the young people within a certain land. Since what has been made easy for them in some lands, from

[6]   Miftah Dar as-Sa'dah: vol. 1 page 442

knowledge, its path, and its study; has not been made possible for others in different lands. But, gather whatever goodness is possible by turning to Allaah, the Most Perfect, for assistance in acquiring the transmitted knowledge from the Prophet, may Allaah's praise and salutations be upon him. As this is what is truly entitled to be called knowledge.

As for other matters besides that, either it is knowledge but it is not truly beneficial, or that which is not actually knowledge but only mistakenly considered to be. Indeed if it actually was beneficial knowledge, then undoubtedly it must be from that which springs from the inherited guidance of Muhammad, may Allaah's praise and salutations be upon him. As there is nothing that can serve in its place as an alternative or substitute, from that which is considered similar to it or seen by some to be better than it.

Therefore, if his purpose and intent is to understand the goals and objectives of the Messenger of Allaah within everything that he commanded and that which he forbade, as well as in the rest of the Messenger's statements; and if his heart becomes satisfied with this understanding and the explanation of the rulings, this is the aim and objective of the Messenger's guidance. ...It is not possible to set straight or rectify the relationship between him and Allaah, the Most High as well as the relationship between him and the people, until he is capable of possessing this understanding. So struggle in every area of the various areas of knowledge to adhere to the foundation and fundamental knowledge which is transmitted directly from the Prophet, may Allaah's praise and salutations be upon him"[7]

[7]   Majmu'a al-Fatawaa: Vol. 19, page 119

Guide to the Symbols for Different Types of Texts or Citations Used with the Book

❖ ❥- (...) indicates a verse of the Qur'aan and the source surah of that verse.

{...}-(...) indicates a narration of the Messenger of Allaah, may Allaah's praise and salutations be upon him, or a narration from one of the first generations or one of the scholars.

The second set of brackets -(...) is where I have in a basic format referenced and indicated some but not all, of its sources as well as its similar supporting narrations, as many times these were not present in the original printed or audio sources. All stated rulings of authenticity are from Imaam al-Albaanee or Imaam Muqbil, may Allaah have mercy upon both of them, according to my limited ability. Similarly I have sometimes mentioned other relevant statements about the referred to narrations from these two distinguished scholars which I found in their books. Lastly, long source citations according to narrator have been separated from the text as numbered footnotes to facilitate reading. It should also be noted that the numbering systems of editions vary widely, and in newer printed or electronic editions the enumeration may differ.

[...] indicates an incorrect statement found among some of the common people or from the callers to falsehood whether from a book or tape.

In this text I have translated the original Arabic expression which is transliterated as, *'salla Allaahu aleihi wa sallam'* in reference to the Messenger of Allaah Muhammad Ibn 'Abdullah, according to the explanation found with the scholars of Ahlus-Sunnah wa al-Jama'ah. Its' meaning is explained in the compilation *'Salafee Selections from the Explanation of Aqeedah al-Waasiteeyah'*. Sheikh al-'Utheimeen, may Allaah the Most High have mercy upon him, stated on pages 114-115,

"As for the meaning of "salla Allaahu aleihi" the most accurate of what has been stated regarding this is what has been related from Abu Aleeyah, may Allaah have mercy upon him: 'It is Allaah's praise and commendation of him among the highest gatherings and assemblies in the heavens.'

...And as for the meaning of "sallam" for him, within it is a statement of his being preserved from errors and shortcomings, and in the statement of "salat" upon him is an affirmation of his realization of the good characteristics and traits... So the single sentence with: "salat' and "sallam' contains an expression that informs but whose meaning is in fact one of asking or requesting by the speaker, as what is intended is supplication to Allaah.'

Sheikh al-Fauzaan, may Allaah preserve, commented on page 116 of that same work:

"And the statement "salla Allaahu aleihi" linguistically carried the meaning of supplication; and the most authentic of what has been stated regarding the meaning of the "salat" from Allaah upon His Messenger is what Imaam al-Bukhaaree mentions in his Saheeh collection from Abu 'Aleeyah that he said: 'It is Allaah's praise and commendation of him among the highest gatherings and assemblies in the heavens.'... and the "sallam" means: salutations of honor or mention of his soundness and freedom from faults and failings'

Therefore within this book its most common transliterated form, "*salla Allaahu aleihi wa sallam*" has been translated as: may Allaah's praise and salutations be upon him, and "*salla Allaahu aleihi wa alaa ahlehe wa sallam*" has been translated as: "may Allaah's praise and salutations be upon him and his household'.

Words of Thanks and Appreciation

I thank Allaah, Glorified and Exalted, for every blessing He has given me. I ask for good mention and prayers and blessings be upon the Prophet of mercy and the Messenger of guidance Muhammad and his family. I wish to thank our esteemed Sheikh Abu Nasr Muhammad Ibn 'Abdullah al-Imaam, may Allaah preserve him, as I occupied his valuable time on more than one occasion, seeking his assistance in the affairs of my deen....

I ask Allaah, Glorified and Exalted, to place me and every Muslim and Muslimah upon the path of beneficial knowledge and righteous actions, and to enable us to walk in the truly successful path as our pious predecessors did so that our knowledge a proof for us and not against us. May Allaah's praise and His salutations be upon our Prophet Muhammad and upon his family and Companions, and all those who follow his guidance until the Day of Judgment. And all praise is due to Allaah, Lord of the Worlds.

Written by Abu Sukhailah
Khalil Ibn-Abelahyi al-Amreekee

(Abridged for Pocket Edition)

(1)

TO THE YOUTH WHO ARE PART OF
TODAY'S REVIVAL OF ISLAAM

direct my letter to all of the youth whom Allaah has granted success in holding firmly to this religion, understanding it, and inviting to it in all of His lands. I advise them to fear Allaah and to confirm matters and proceed carefully in their affairs avoiding hastiness. Similarly, I advise them to devote themselves to the Noble Qur'aan, its recitation, its contemplation, its memorization, and its review and study.

Likewise I advise them to adhere to the Sunnah of the Messenger of Allaah, may Allaah's praise and His salutations be upon him, memorizing its texts, giving attention to it and studying it well. In the same manner, to study the books of sound authentic beliefs, the beliefs of the people who cling to the Sunnah and the body of the Muslims who are united upon the truth. For example, *((Kitaab at-Tawheed)06-01)* *((Thalaathatul Usul)06-02)*, and *((Kashf ash-Shubahaat)06-04)* of Sheikh Muhammad Ibn 'Abdul-Wahaab may Allaah have mercy upon him. Also the books *((at-Tadrumeeyah)06-07)*, *((al-Hamaweeyah)06-06)*, *((al-Aqeedatul-Wasateeyah)06-05)* of Sheikh al-Islaam Ibn Taymeeyah, may Allaah have mercy upon him. And such as *((al-Qaseedat an-Nooneeyah)06-15)*, *((as-Sawa'aiq al-Mursalah)12-04)*, *((Ighathatul al-Lahfaan min Makaa'id as-Shaytaan)12-05)*, *((Zaad al-Ma'ad Fee Haadee Khair al-Ebaad)09-05)*, *((Ijtimaa' al-Jawaish al-Islaameeyah)06-16)* from the major scholar Ibn al-Qayyim, may Allaah have mercy upon him. And the book, *((Lama't al-Itiqaad)06-13)* from Muwafiq Ibn Qudaamah may Allaah have mercy upon him, and *((al-Muqadamah)12-06)* of Abee Zayd al-Qeeruwaanee al-Maalikee, may Allaah Have mercy upon him. As well as similar works from books of correct belief written by the scholars well known for their knowledge, merit, and true beliefs. Additionally, for example the book *((Kitaab at-Tawheed)06-36)* of Ibn Khuzaymah, may Allaah have mercy upon him, and *((Kitaab as-Sunnah)06-22)* from 'Abdullah

Ibn Ahmad Ibn Hanbal, as well as other books similar to them.

I advise them with concern for the call to Allaah, enjoining the good and forbidding wrong with wisdom, excellent behavior, and good speech. They should proceed not with harshness and severity, but rather with gentleness and insight, as Allaah, Glorified and Exalted says, ❧*Invite (mankind, Oh Muhammad) to the Way of your Lord (i.e. Islaam) with wisdom (i.e. with the Divine Inspiration and the Qur'aan) and fair preaching, and argue with them in a way that is better.*❧-(Surah an-Nahl:125). And He, Glorified be He, said, ❧*And by the Mercy of Allaah, you dealt with them gently. And had you been severe and harsh-hearted, they would have broken away from about you.* ❧-(Surah Aal-'Imraan:159)

I advise them to avoid hastiness in every matter. Rather, they should ascertain matters carefully, consult others, and cooperate upon goodness until they understand the religion properly, as the Messenger, may Allaah's praise and His salutations be upon him, said, *{The one whom Allaah intends good for He gives him understanding in the religion}* [1].

Indeed hastiness leads to tremendous harm. Thus, it is an obligation to verify matters and give attention to the Sharee'ah evidences, and to always frequent the sittings of knowledge of those people of knowledge well known for their uprightness and sound beliefs.

---

[1]   Narrated in Saheeh al-Bukhaaree: 71, 3116, 7312/ Saheeh Muslim: 1037/ Sunan Ibn Maajah: 221/ al-Muwatta Maalik: 1300, 1667/ & Musnad Imaam Ahmad: 16395: 16404, and other than these two/ Musannaf Ibn Abee Shaybah: 31792/ & Sunan ad-Daaramee: 224, 226/ - on the authority of Mu'aweeyah. And it is found in Jaame' al-Tirmidhee: 2645/ Musnad Imaam Ahmad: 2786/ & Sunan ad-Daaramee: 270, 2706/-on the authority of Ibn 'Abbaas. And it is found in Sunan Ibn Maajah:220/ & Musannaf 'Abdul-Razzaaq: 30851/-on the authority of Abu Hurairah. It was declared authentic by Sheikh al-Albaanee in Saheeh al-Aadab al-Mufrad: 517, Silsilat al-Hadeeth as-Saheehah: 1194, 1195, 1196, Saheeh at-Targheeb at-Tarheeb: 67, as well as in other of his books. Sheikh Muqbil declared it authentic in al-Jaame' al-Saheeh: 9, 3123, 4650, may Allaah have mercy upon them both.

To the Scholars and Students of Knowledge

I advise the scholars and the students of knowledge collectively to fear Allaah, and be concerned with the verification of issues of knowledge through Sharee'ah evidences, not through simply blindly following this person or that person. And I advise all of you to devote yourselves to the Book of Allaah and the Sunnah of the Messenger, may Allaah's praise and salutations be upon him, and to refer back to the clarifying words of the scholars, until you comprehend the truth by its evidences, not merely by unconditionally accepting the speech of this individual or blindly following that person.

Likewise, I advise the students of knowledge to continue to strive to understand this religion, to derive knowledge from the Sharee'ah evidences, as well as to cooperate upon goodness and the fear of Allaah and advise others to hold to the truth and be patient upon that. I advise them to spread knowledge among the people in the masjids as well as outside of the masjids in other locations, in their sermons, lessons, sittings of knowledge, in the schools and universities- in any place they may be. I ask Allaah to grant all of us success, and to rectify both our intentions and our actions.

[FROM 'COLLECTION OF RULINGS AND VARIOUS STATEMENTS': VOL. 6, PAGE 232]

(2)

QUESTION: THERE IS SPREADING THROUGHOUT THE MUSLIM WORLD A BLESSED ISLAMIC REVIVAL WHICH ALL MUSLIMS WELCOME AND ARE PLEASED WITH. HOWEVER, WE SEE THAT THIS REVIVAL DOES NOT PLACE SUFFICIENT CONCERN AND EMPHASIS ON THE CORRECT UNDERSTANDING OF SHAREE'AH MATTERS, NOR UPON THE FUNDAMENTALS OF THE CORRECT BELIEFS OF ISLAAM. WHAT IS YOUR ADVICE, ESTEEMED SCHOLAR, IN RELATION TO THIS REVIVAL?

nswer: My advice to all of the Muslims- the Muslim youth as well as to the elders, the men and the women- my advice to all of them is to give attention to the Book of Allaah, the Noble Qur'aan. Focus upon its recitation, its contemplation, thinking about it and acting according to it, and asking about any matter they do not understand. Also that they refer to and read the reliable books in the field of explanations of the meaning of the Qur'aan, such as the books of *((Ibn Jareer)01-04)*, *((Ibn Katheer)01-01)*, *((al-Baghawee)01-07)*, and other reliable books from the works which explain the Qur'aan. This is in order that they will be able to understand the meanings of the Word of Allaah and be steadfast upon that which the Book of Allaah guides to from the matters of worshipping Allaah alone without partners; have sincerity towards Him alone, establishing all its requirements or affairs, and leaving that which negates it. Along with this, one should give attention to the books authored regarding the beliefs held by the first three generations of righteous Muslims such as *((Kitaab at-Tawheed)06-01)*, *((Thalatatul-Usul)06-02)*, and *((Kashf as-Shubahaat)06-13)* by the Sheikh Muhammad Ibn 'Abdul-Wahhab, may Allaah have mercy upon him. Also *((al-Aqeedat al-Wasatiyyah)06-05)* of the Sheikh Ibn Taymeeyah, *((Lama't al-Itiqaad)06-13)* of Imaam al-Muwafiq Ibn Qudaamah and *((Sharh at-Tahaweeyah)06-09)* of Ibn Abee al-Izz, and written works similar to them which are well known to proceed upon the methodology of the people of the Sunnah.

Additionally, the summarized books of hadeeth narrations such as *((Arba'een an-Nawawee)02-27)* and *((the supplement)03-09)* which completes it by Ibn Rajab, *((Amdatul-Hadeeth)02-29)* by Sheikh 'Abdul-Ghanee al-Maqdasee, and *((Bulugh al-Maraam)02-34)* by Ibn Hajr. Haafidh Ibn Hajr also has a beneficial work related to hadeeth science terminology, *((Nukhbat al-Fikr)04-01)*, as well as *((his own explanation)04-02)* of this book.

Similarly in the principles of jurisprudence, or deriving the understanding of the texts, refer to the book, *((Rawdhat an-Naadher)08-08)* of Muwaafiq Ibn Qudaamah.

So what is intended by all of this is giving attention to the fundamentals in the subject of correct belief, to the fundamentals of the science of deriving the correct understanding from the source texts, and the fundamentals of the hadeeth sciences and terminology. These would benefit them, and it is these fundamentals that the various areas of knowledge are built upon.

Likewise in the area of compiled works of fiqh rulings, *(('Amdat al-Fiqh)07-03)* of Muwafiq Ibn Qudammah, *((Zaad al-Mustaqna')07-01)* of Hajaawee, and *((Daleel at-Taalib)07-23)*. These books benefit and are useful to the student of knowledge, in as far as they will help him comprehend various issues, their related evidences, as well as the sources or references which are relied upon. All of these are matters of importance for the student of knowledge.

FROM 'COLLECTION OF RULINGS AND VARIOUS STATEMENTS': VOL.8, PAGES 232-233]

(3)

QUESTIONS: WE WOULD LIKE YOU TO EXPLAIN THE MEANING OF ALLAAH'S STATEMENT, ❁VERILY THOSE WHO FEAR AND HAVE REVERENCE OF ALLAAH THE MOST FROM HIS WORSHIPERS ARE THE SCHOLARS❁

nswer: This is a tremendous verse, and indicates that the scholars of Allaah, of His religion, of His exalted Book, and of the Sunnah of His noble Messenger are the strongest of the people in standing in awe and reverence of Allaah, and those most complete in fearing Him, the Most Free from Imperfections. Its meaning is that those who have awe and reverence for Allaah in a true and complete manner, they are the scholars of Allaah, who know their Lord by His names and attributes, and who exalt and magnify Him. They are those who consider carefully the matters of his Sharee'ah, and those who understand the bounty that will be found with Him from happiness for those who fear Him, as well as the punishment for those to turn away from Him and His guidance and commit sin and transgression. And they are those who, due to the comprehensiveness of their knowledge of Him, are the strongest of the people in having true reverence of Him and the most complete of the people in having fear of Him.

At the head of them are the Messengers and the Prophets, upon them all be praise and salutations, as they are the most complete of the people in standing in awe and reverence of Allaah, the Most Free from Imperfection, and in glorifying Him. After them, then those who succeeded and followed them, meaning the scholars of Allaah and His religion. And the people are categorized according to different levels, as the verses do not mean that others who are not scholars do not fear Allaah, as every Muslim and Muslimah, every believing man and believing woman fears Allaah the Most High, the Most Exalted. Rather, it is that the fearing of Allaah among them is in varying degrees, and whenever the believer is more perceptive and conscious of Allaah and the more knowledgeable about Allaah and His religion, then his fear of Allaah will increase. Whenever his knowledge and perception decreases, then his fear of Allaah, reverence and awe of Allaah, the Most Perfect also decreases.

So the people vary greatly in regard to their levels, such that even the scholars are of different levels in their reverence and awe, as was discussed. So whenever they are increased in knowledge then their awe of Allaah increases and likewise, whenever their knowledge decreases this diminishes their awe and reverence of Allaah. And due to this the Most High and Most Exalted says,

Verily, those who disbelieve from among the people of the Scripture and those who associate others with Allaah will abide in the Fire of Hell. They are the worst of creatures. Verily, those who believe and do righteous good deeds, they are the best of creatures. Their reward with their Lord is 'Adn Paradise, underneath which rivers flow, they will abide therein forever, Allaah Well-Pleased with them, and they with Him. That is for him who fears his Lord.-(Surah al-Baiyyinah:6-8) And Allaah, the Most High, says, *Verily! Those who fear their Lord unseen, theirs will be forgiveness and a great reward*-(Surah al-Mulk: 12). And the verses with this meaning are many, and from Allaah is the success.

[FROM 'A COLLECTION OF RULINGS AND VARIOUS STATEMENTS': VOL.5, PAGE 48]

(4)

THE REASONS FOR THE WEAKNESS OF THE MUSLIMS IN THE FACE OF THEIR ENEMIES AND THE MEANS TO CURE THIS

answer: The Reasons for the Weakness of the Muslims in the Face of their Enemies and the Means to Cure This.

All praise is for Allaah Lord of all the Worlds, the final destination of those who fear and revere Him, and praise and salutations be upon His worshiper and Messenger, and the One entrusted with His revelation, the best of His creation, our Prophet, leader, and chief, Muhammad Ibn 'Abdullah Ibn 'Abdul-Mutalib and also upon his Companions and those who travel upon his path and those who follow his guidance until the Day Of Reckoning. As for what follows:

Certainly concern has been shown by the prominent Muslim thinkers and intellectuals, those who are associated with the present Islamic revival, and the individuals who contemplate matters seriously, for the circumstances which the Muslims find themselves in. Without question, they have occupied themselves with this matter a great deal, and considered at length the reasons for the weakness of the Muslims, the causes for their inferior position in front of their enemies, and the reasons for their divisiveness and disunity. In addition, they have contemplated the reasons for the arrogance of their enemies in relation to them, such that they have even taken control of some of their lands. Subsequently, after they have understood the causes and reasons, and these reasons are evident, then importance must be given to determining the cure and solution required to remedy the causes which have inevitably led to our disgrace and weakness. And this solution is also known. However, what is necessary is that it be publicized and explained clearly. This is because recognizing the illness and then determining the cure is from the most significant means leading to successful treatment and health.

The one with an illness, when he understands the illness as well as understanding the cure, is best capable of beginning to utilize the cure and free himself from that illness. And it is natural for the intelligent person who prefers life and freedom from illness to give importance to recognizing the illness and knowing its cure. However, some of the people have been overtaken by the disease and overwhelmed by it until they become satisfied with it, and pleased with it, until their perception and awareness has died. Thus they do not pay attention to the one who explains to them the remedy, as the illness itself has become normal and natural to them. They are comfortable and content to remain in a corrupted state of mind, having a weak perception, along with the domination of their desires over them; their intellects, hearts, and conduct. And this has happened to the majority of people in relation to the illness and deficiency in their practice of the religion and the cure for it. And most people are thus content, preferring to remain in a miserable condition and state of sickness which weakens them and prevents any attempt to truly recognize the illness, its consequences, and what will result from it immediately and long term, as well as preventing efforts to search for a cure, or desiring that, even when it is clearly described and explained to them, and close at hand. They do not give any importance to this. With this comes the worsening of the sickness, the further satisfaction with its presence, the concealment of its harm upon them, and the lack of strong determination to understand the significance of the problem.

And so the causes for the weakness of the Muslims and their present inferior position has been explained by the scholars, the people of intelligence, and the leaders possessing true insight into and knowledge of the nations in this age and the periods preceding it. In addition, they have clarified the means to the effective remedy, its results and outcome, if the remedy is properly used.

So the reasons for the weakness, inferiority, and domination of our enemies return back to a primary cause from which proceed many other causes, and from a single factor from which many other factors spring. The primary cause and single factor is ignorance. Ignorance of Allaah and His religion, and the consequences of this ignorance which have overtaken the majority of them, such that the present state has become one where knowledge is rare and this ignorance widespread. Then from this ignorance stems further causes and factors, such as love of the worldly life and a hatred of death, and the negligence of prayer and the following of desires. From these is the lack of preparation for confrontation with their enemies and being pleased to have their needs supplied by their enemies, and a failure to give high priority to the producing of goods for their essential needs from their own lands and resources. Also stemming from this is division and differing, the lack of having a united voice, and lack of unity and cooperation. So from these dangerous causes and their results has come about that which is seen of weakness in the face of our enemies and our inferiority in every matter except that which Allaah has willed, as well as the devotion to prohibited desires, and becoming occupied with matters that hinder efforts in the path of Allaah and guidance, not to mention the lack of preparing to confront our enemies, either from the aspect of means of production, or in terms of sufficient weaponry that would intimidate the enemy and is needed to fight and struggle against him, and take what is a right from him.

In addition, there is the lack of preparing our bodies for jihaad and the failure to use our wealth on what is necessary to prepare in strength of numbers for the enemy, to protect against the harm they may bring forth, and to be able to defend both the religion and the land.

Also proceeding from this sickness is the striving to obtain worldly things by every possible way, and to gather them by every means, so that every individual becomes someone who only gives importance to serving himself and is not truly connected to his land. Through this state of affairs, his religion, or the majority of it, basically fades away. This is in fact the general condition and what is prevalent in most of the states or countries associated with the religion of Islaam today. Rather, it is more accurate that we say that this has occurred everywhere except where Allaah, the Most High, the Most Sublime, decreed that some efforts of preparation and protection are being made; however not in a complete way that fulfills all the desired aspects of rectification.

['COLLECTION OF RULINGS AND VARIOUS STATEMENTS': VOL. 5, PAGE 101]

(5)

QUESTION: WHAT IS YOUR VIEW OF THE SAYING FOUND ON THE TONGUES OF MANY STUDENTS OF KNOWLEDGE THAT, "THE ONE WHOSE TEACHER IS HIS BOOK, HIS ERRORS ARE GREATER THAT WHICH HE IS CORRECT IN"

nswer: It is well known that the one whose sole teacher is his book, then his mistakes are more numerous than the matters he is correct in. This is the expression which we know, and it is correct, as the one who does not study with the people of knowledge, does not take knowledge from them, and does not understand the path that they have passed upon in seeking knowledge, certainly makes many errors. Also, it may be unclear and doubtful to him the difference between what is right and what is wrong or incorrect regarding specific issues, as he has not fully understood the Sharee'ah evidences, nor the established methods which the people of knowledge have made use of; meaning those which they had utilized and acted upon in making such determinations.

As to whether his mistakes will be more numerous than what they are correct in, then this is something debatable. But in any case he will make many mistakes, as he did not learn from the people of knowledge nor benefit from them. Thus, he does not understand the principles which must be utilized in reaching conclusions, and therefore makes many mistakes. Additionally, he cannot distinguish between mistakes and what is correct within printed and manuscript books, as an error will appear in a book and he does not have the familiarity and ability to recognize that, and so believes it to be correct. He then may give a ruling of permissibility for that which Allaah has forbidden, or declare forbidden that which Allaah has made permissible, because he lacks insight. This occurs simply because of a printing or writing error that he came across in a book.

For example, it may state, "*Such and such is not permissible.*" while what is correct from the original text is that states that it is permissible, as there is may be an unwarranted addition to the text of that printing which is an error. Or the opposite where it says, "*Such and such is permissible*" while what is correct in the original text is that it states that it is not permissible. This would be caused by an omission in that specific printing or line, and this is a tremmistake. Similar is the expression: "*...what is correct is such-and-such*", while what is actually correct is that is stated "*... what is not correct is such-and-such*". So he would get confused in this because of his lack of perceptiveness and knowledge and so does not recognize an error that may be present in a book, or situations similar to this.

[FROM 'A COLLECTION OF RULINGS AND VARIOUS STATEMENTS': VOL. 7, PAGE 243]

(6)

QUESTION: SOME PEOPLE HOLD THE VIEW THAT IT IS NECESSARY THAT EFFORTS OF CALLING TO ALLAAH ONLY BE IN THE MASJIDS. WHAT IS YOUR POSITION REGARDING THIS? AND WHICH ENVIRONMENTS AND METHODS ARE ACCEPTABLE IN THE ISSUE OF CALLING TO ALLAAH?

nswer: In the name of Allaah, all praise is due to Allaah. Calling to Allaah is not limited masjids only. There are clearly other locations and means that are also related to it. There is no doubt that the masjids hold opportunities for calling to Allaah, such as during the day of Jumu'ah sermon, and other sermons, and preaching around the times of the prayers, and circles of learning. So the masjid is the foundation for the spreading of knowledge and the religion. However, calling to Allaah is not restricted to the masjid alone.

The caller to Allaah also invites in places other than the masjids, such as at any suitable gatherings as well as at casual gatherings. So the believers should seize the opportunities to call to Allaah by way of the different forms of modern media, and also by means of written works. All of these are from the ways of calling to Allaah. The intelligent person seizes the opportunities at every time and place where it is possible to call and invite, putting forth as much effort as he is able in calling to Allaah with wisdom, good speech, and excellent behavior.

[FROM 'COLLECTION OF RULINGS AND VARIOUS STATEMENTS':
VOL. 8, PAGE 407]

(7)

THE IDEOLOGICAL WAR: ITS CHARACTERISTICS, METHODS AND THE REQUIRED RESPONSE TO IT

All praise is due to Allaah, and Allaah's praise and salutation be upon the Messenger of Allaah, his family, his Companions, and those who follow their guidance. As for what follows:

The Lord, the Most High and Exalted, sent the Messengers, upon them be Allaah's blessings and salutations, with that which encompasses contentment and success for the world both in this life and the life of the Hereafter. He made them a mercy for His worshipers. He guided them and then guided others through them to the truth; and through them He takes people out of darkness into light. He made our prophet Muhammad the best of them, their leader, and the final Messenger, may Allaah's praise and salutations be upon him. He sent the guidance and the religion of truth so that it may dominate over all the paths, as Allaah, the Exalted and Most High, said in His clear book, ❃*It is He Who has sent His Messenger (Muhammad) with guidance and the religion of truth*❃-(Surah Tawbah:33)

'Guidance' means that which Allaah sent him with from beneficial types of knowledge, true information, an admonishment which gives life to the hearts, and narrations of past events which remind the worshipers of what will reach the people of faith in Allaah from contentment, and of what will reach the people of disbelief and falsehood from misery, disastrous consequences, and evil. The religion of truth is that which Allaah sent the Messenger with: Allaah revealed laws whose only origin is heaven, the rulings of how to live, and beneficial teachings that guide. He calls to Allaah, the Most High, the Most Exalted, by giving good tidings and warnings, and informing the people of how they may achieve success and happiness while conveying everything to them with a clear explanation. And his Lord did not send him except that His religion would be completed by His Messenger's hand, and that He would perfect His blessing through him, may the best of his Lord's blessings and salutations be upon him.

The subject of the seminar tonight is "*The Ideological War*", and I hope that the noble attendees who undertake consideration of this topic are able to acheive and effectively examination of this subject. We ask Allaah for them, ourselves, and all the Muslims, well-being and success.

The ideological warfare which has been examined and discussed by the scholars, is that which has become pervasive and has spread through the majority of publications, newspapers, and other written works; it encompasses everything that has been spread through the world is that which is clearly related to ideology, concepts, and beliefs. As the enemies of Islaam, when they became infuriated with the continued prominence and emergence of Islaam, and witnessed the people continuing to enter into the religion of Allaah in significant numbers, as well as their seeing the failure of their attempts at military force used to achieve the goal of causing the people to unsure and doubtful about their religion, thereafter in order to further attempt to pull them away from Islaam; then they resorted to different forms and types of ideological warfare by means of various forms of modern media such as television, publications, newspapers, and other written and spoken content produced and developed by those who oppose Islaam. They utilize these in their efforts to hinder and repel the religion of Allaah, and spread uncertainty amongst the people regarding the religion, covering the truth with deceptions and falsehood. This is similar to what Allaah states regarding those who opposed Him from amongst the Jews, where the Most High, Most Exalted says, ❪*And mix not truth with falsehood, nor conceal the truth while you know the truth*❫-(Surah al-Baqarah:42)

The modern forms of media which those who oppose Islaam have established produce damage of every type, and every form of trial and ordeal, while obstructing and hindering every matter related to the truth. They invite to that which is falsehood, while slipping poison within the delightfulness and fullness of what is offered. They have in mind through this way to cause people to have doubts and uncertainties about the correctness of the religion; all in order to pull them out from the light of Allaah and His guidance, towards the darkness of disbelief and misguidance, to turn them away from the truth and encourages them towards misguidance. And what is sufficient initially is that doubt, misgivings, and distance from the truth result from their efforts.

Then they follow up and build upon that with efforts by corrupt and ignorant Muslims, who spread corrupt ideas and mistaken beliefs and ideologies, such that now they, the Muslims, are then surrounded with various forms of falsehood after having been previously prevented from perceiving the truth.

All of this is from what Shaytaan invites to and propagates, as is found in the statement of the Most High, ❖*Surely, Shaytaan is an enemy to you, so take (treat) him as an enemy. He only invites his followers that they may become the dwellers of the blazing Fire.*❖-(Surah Faater: 6). And regarding his party, meaning Shaytaan's- know that the disbelievers of Islaam and every individual who calls to that which obstructs the truth and encourages falsehood- is a supporter of Shaytaan's party.

It is seen that in some instances of their efforts, they would invite to or promote adultery and indecency in its various forms, while at other times they do so through publishing and spreading the images of women.

At other times, they promote the display of women's physical beauty and its exposure in the most beautiful forms in order to push young men and others towards indecency, while at other times, by spreading corrupt beliefs and concepts which negate or remove Islaam.

And at times, they plant doubts about that which the Messengers of Allaah came with, Allaah's praise and salutations be upon them; bringing forth uncertainties that confuse even an intelligent person.

All of these matters are part of the call of the enemies of Allaah, and they are the close associates of Shaytaan in his party.

Therefore it is obligatory upon every person of intelligence and every individual who desires safety and protection to look towards the path and way which would distance himself from this current or movement of increasing corruption and from this destructive assault which produces doubt and uncertainties, so that he may stay firmly upon the path of contentment and success in hopes that he will be successful.

This is especially true in our age, in which there are many false ideological calls, and in which there are many forms of falsehood, which have been disseminated and spread, and various types of assaults of corruption and heretical concepts circulated. The world is saturated with writings, which obstruct people from the truth; and those close to the enemies of Allaah have writers engaged in preventing the spreading of the truth by producing such materials for the various forms of print media. Similarly, within the various forms of audio and visual media, there is constantly circulated day and night material which prevents and turns people away from the truth and preoccupies them from that which would benefit and guide them. Anyone who has the most basic understanding of these methods, and what is spread through them by the enemies of Allaah in the newspapers in various languages, know that the lands of Islaam and the Muslims specifically are being attacked by various types of calls and different categories of misguided heretical concepts to turn them away from the path of Allaah. It includes calls to take on aspects of blameworthy or evil character and characteristics and characteristics which Allaah has forbidden His servants to have and possess, and to cause them to hate and turn away from aspects of praiseworthy or good character and righteous actions and endeavors.

So it is a requirement upon every believing man and upon every believing woman to be warned about these deceitful and dangerous methods, either by responding by refuting them or by explaining their falsehood and warning from them. This along with calling the people to turn to and give priority to the Book of their Lord, as it is the foundation of contentment and happiness and the source and well of knowledge. It is the strongest of fortresses for the one who hold firmly to it in protection from the various forms of misguidance. As Allaah, the Most High and the Most Exalted, says in His tremendous Book, ❖*Verily, this Qur'aan guides to that which is most just and right.*❖-(Surah al-Israa': 9) And the One free from faults says ❖*Say: It is for those who believe, a guide and a healing.*❖-(Surah Fussilat:44) He also says, ❖*This is a Book which We have sent down to you, full of blessings; that they may ponder over its Verses, and that men of understanding may remember*❖-(Surah Saad:29) And the One free from faults says, ❖*And this is a blessed Book which We have sent down, so follow it and fear Allaah, that you may receive mercy*❖-(Surah al-Ana'am:155) And the One free from faults says, ❖*Verily, those who disbelieved in the Reminder when it came to them shall receive the punishment. And verily, it is an honorable respected Book. Falsehood cannot come to it from before it or behind it. It is sent down by the All-Wise, Worthy of all praise*❖-(Surah Fussilat:42) As well as of the verses which guide to His tremendous Book, which He has made a guidance and a means of happiness for all of mankind. It is obligatory upon the people of Faith to hold firmly to this book by frequently reciting it and carefully pondering its meanings, as the diseases of the heart, as well as the problems of society, are rectified by this tremendous Book. Along with this, they should produce materials that are related to it, publishing and distributing them by means of various publications, television, and various types of authored works such as small but beneficial introductory or summarized writings which guide to the truth. This is defending Allaah's religion as well as spreading it, and refuting the misguided statements and those writings which plant doubts and uncertainty which are being spread in distributed through every available means by the enemies of Allaah.

In regards to the Sunnah of the Messenger, may Allaah's praise and salutations be upon him, Allaah has made it a source of guidance for the people and the guiding light for the one who holds firmly to it, an explanation to the Book of Allaah, and a clarification to matters which are explained in a basic or simple form in the book of Allaah. Just as Allaah, the Most High and Most Exalted says ❖*We have also sent down unto you the reminder and the advice, that you may explain clearly to men what is sent down to them, and that they may give thought.*❖-(Surah an-Nahl:44) Allaah, the Most High and Most Exalted, says, ❖*By the star when it goes down, (or vanishes). Your companion Muhammad has neither gone astray nor has erred. Nor does he speak of his own desire. It is only an Inspiration that is inspired.*❖-(Surah an-Najm:1-4) This is Muhammad, upon him be Allaah's praise and salutations. ❖*Your companion has neither gone astray....*❖ meaning Muhammad, upon him be Allaah's praise and salutations, "... nor has he erred." The one who is "astray" is the one who speaks without guidance, from other than true knowledge. Additionally, the one who "has erred" is the one who opposes knowledge; one who understands but still opposes knowledge, like the Jews, and those like them. Similarly, the evil scholars who comprehend the truth but deviate away from it towards falsehood due to giving preference to their desires, and preference to the world and worldly pleasures. Allaah frees and clears his Prophet from this, may Allaah's praise and salutations be upon him, stating clearly that he is not astray, nor one who has fallen into error; rather he is knowledgeable and guided, may Allaah's praise and salutations be upon him. He is the one who understands the truth, calls to it, and is established firmly upon it. Allaah has made him a noble Messenger who guides and is himself guided; who was a warner away from falsehood for the people and the one who brings the glad tidings of the truth: *Oh Prophet! Verily, We have sent you as witness, and a bearer of glad tidings, and a warner. And as one who invites to Allaah by His Leave, and as a lamp spreading light.*-(Surah al-Ahzab:45-46) May Allaah's praise and salutations be upon him.

He lived in this world after receiving the call to prophethood for twenty-three years, all of which were spent calling to Allaah, teaching, and guiding others by speech and action. All of that time he was striving patiently with his body, and tongue, as well as militarily. Thirteen of these years were within Mecca; calling, guiding, and leading to the truth, being patient with all harm and hardship, guiding the people to goodness by his speech and actions, may Allaah's praise and salutations be upon him. As well as ten years in Medinah, striving militarily and striving with his tongue, and striving through his actions, guiding his companions to goodness, may Allaah be pleased and contented with them, until Allaah completed through them his religion, and perfected His blessing upon them. Therefore it is obligatory upon every individual who wants success and safety, and every individual who wishes for himself honor and desires contentment, to adhere to these two forms of revelation: the Book of Allaah and the Sunnah of the Messenger of Allaah, upon him be Allaah's praise and salutations. He must hold fast to both of them, invite to them, give concern and priority to memorizing them and contemplating them, spreading what they contain of knowledge while acting according to that knowledge and inviting others to act according to it.

Allaah blessed the companions of His Prophet and they held firmly to that and established themselves upon the Book and the Sunnah, may Allaah be pleased with them. They strove in the path of Allaah, and were victorious in many conquests, and founded new cities. They fought against the Romans and the Persians and other disbelieving nations, defeating them and spreading Islaam in their lands. They took the jizyah tax from those Jews, Christians, and Magians who chose not to embrace Islaam. They called to Allaah in speech and action, being patient with the harm and struggle until Allaah raised up His religion, gave victory to His religion through them, elevated His word, and spread the truth through them. This is the way of the companions of the Prophet, may Allaah's praise and salutations be upon him, and the way of the one who proceeds upon their path, the one who shares with them this tremendous struggle and the call to Allaah, the Most High and the Most Exalted. The friends of Allaah and those who support them in the call to Allaah and struggle in His path did not cease their efforts until the conditions changed and there began to enter into Islaam those who were not Muslims. But from the ones who call to falsehood there has occurred what has occurred from the gathering and emergence of various forms of misguidance, until the conditions become like those which we find ourselves within today; evil being predominant with numerous callers to falsehood, and tremendous activity from the direction of the lands of the disbelievers, and weakness in the Muslim states, and their failure to rule by the Sharee'ah except to a small degree. This is because most of them are pleased with the laws devised by men and devised by the enemies of Allaah, while they forsake the Sharee'ah of Allaah. So there has spread in these lands corruption, evil, and misguidance due to their turning away and their inactivity and sluggishness upon the truth; as well as their lack of patience and spreading and calling to the truth, and struggling against those who oppose the truth, until the present situation in which misguidance has emerged and proliferated and is widespread. It is therefore obligatory to call to the most fundamental of foundations: to the book of Allaah and the Sunnah of the Messenger of Allaah, as these two foundations are that which the struggle of the Messenger of Allaah was based upon. Likewise, the noble companions and those who followed them in goodness also struggled upon these two foundations. There is no way to reach contentment and success in the face of this ideological warfare, or victory over our enemies, except by adhering firmly to these two foundations: the book of Allaah and the Sunnah of the Messenger of Allaah, upon him be Allaah's praise and salutations. We must unite upon them, and cooperate in our speech, actions, writings, struggles, and other than that from the various endeavors which give victory to the truth and invite to it, while opposing, suppressing, and exposing misguidance.

They Appeared among the Muslims, and all praise is due to Allaah, in the beginning of this century and in the previous century called and invited to the truth, and made tremendous efforts in calling to Allaah, the Most High and the Most Exalted. There emerged righteous young men who were committed to adhering to the book of Allaah and the Sunnah of the Messenger of Allaah, upon him be Allaah's praise and salutations. They were also supported in that by the scholars and the people of knowledge, and the virtuous people from their elders and their youth, until all praise is due to Allaah, the appearance or manifestation of the success of Allaah's religion. It was given new life against falsehood, and the many people of falsehood. However, their example was stated by the Prophet, may Allaah's praise and salutations be upon him, when he said, *{There will not cease to be a group from my Ummah victorious upon the truth. They are not harmed by those who oppose them, or those that leave them* *until Allaah's judgment comes.}* [1]. And they, all praise is due to Allaah, are still active, and increase in good; and there has spread through the different countries of the world, to the ends of the earth, the invitation to the truth and guiding the creation. They were graduates from the Islamic University, schools, institutes, and circles of study; and in every location, they spread the truth, calling to it in opposition to the people of misguidance. This situation infuriated enemies of Allaah, and was the reason for them to increase their endeavors of misguidance and the reason for the state of dismay and agitation that we see from them. But we ask Allaah to give victory to His religion and to elevate His word, and that He grant success to all the Muslims, the young and the old, causing them to cooperate and join forces in aiding the truth and to support and assist those who are striving to establish it. We ask that He give victory to them all over the enemies of Allaah, and that He assist them in their striving against Allaah's enemies with the sword and the arrow as well as by the proof and evidence, and to make steadfast the people of the truth upon the truth that is with them. We ask that He guides the Muslim rulers to establish the truth and aid it towards victory, and to rule by the Sharee'ah of Allaah in their affairs until the Supporter grants them victory. We ask that He assist them against their enemies, and that He grants them strength in the goodness they possess, and that they become defended against the plans and plots of Allaah's enemies. As He is the Most High and the Most Exalted, the Bountiful and the Generous.

---

[1]   Narrated in Saheeh al-Bukhaaree: 3641, 7460/ Saheeh Muslim: 1037/ & Musnad Imaam Ahmad: 16785/ -on the authority of Mu'aweeyah. And it is found in Saheeh Muslim: 1920/ & Musnad Imaam Ahmad: 21897/ -on the authority of Tawbaan Ibn Bejadded. And it is found in Jaame'a at-Tirmidhee: 2192/ Sunan Ibn Maajah:6/ & Musnad Imaam Ahmad: 19849/ -on the authority of Qurrah Ibn Ayaas. It was declared authentic by Sheikh al-Albaanee in Silsilat al-Hadeeth as-Saheehah: 1957. Sheikh Muqbil declared it authentic in al-Jaame'a al-Saheeh: 2384.

It is an obligation upon every student of knowledge, wherever they are, to make every effort and truly strive to give victory to the truth, and upon every scholar, wherever he may be, to make every effort and truly strive to give victory to the truth. As this age is the age of calling and invitation; this is the age of jihaad by speaking and spreading the truth, of calling to it by writing, calling, sermons, and other methods from the types of jihaad by the pen and the tongue; by striving and working to guide, by giving advice individually and collectively in speeches, as well as other means. In this way, jihaad is established. In this way, the scholar and the student of knowledge, wherever he may be in his land or other than his land, should be among those who spread the truth and call to it, patiently hoping for Allaah's reward, seeking His Face and pleasure and the life of the next world. They should spread the truth by means of the different forms of the media whenever possible, according to what is facilitated for them from deliberateness and surety, with close attention being giving to properly understanding the truth, because speech without knowledge and understanding harms tremendously. So it is necessary to have understanding, and necessary to have knowledge, as Allaah, the Most High says,

❖*Say: "This is my way; I invite unto Allaah with sure knowledge*❖-(Surah Yusuf:108). Indeed, it is prohibited to speak without knowledge. It is upon the scholars and the callers to explain and follow the truth, and to struggle to expose falsehood and suppress it, as well to shield the Muslims from this assault which has been established from many fronts- within publications, television, newspapers, various writings, congregational prayer sermons, marriage sermons, and similar means. This is because every matter is to be opposed by that which is similar to it; so falsehood is combated by that which is similar to it, according to one's capacity, location, and circumstances. Due to this, the scholar, the student of knowledge, and the believer must actively engage in those matters which Allaah has obligated upon him. It is not proper for the intelligent person to see himself as insignificant, as is found in the hadeeth, *{No one should belittle himself, or see something done for Allaah's sake as insignificant, and so not speak..}* [2] or as he actually stated, upon him be Allaah's praise and salutations. It is required that the student of knowledge speak with that which is learned of truth upon understanding, specifically when falsehood has penetrated into every place and the general affairs have become obscure and confused. Allaah, the Most High, Most Exalted, is the One who sent down the Book to clarify every matter. As he, the One free from any defects says, *◈And We have sent down to you the Book as an exposition of everything, a guidance, a mercy, and glad tidings for those who have submitted themselves to Allaah as Muslims.◈*-(Surah an-Nahl:89) This tremendous book is the Qur'aan, containing both proofs and clarification; a guidance and clarification of the path to contentment, as well as containing a refutation, opposition, and suppression of misguidance. It is not permissible for the scholar to be satisfied with remaining silent, or to be satisfied with doing less than he is truly capable of, regardless of where he is; whether he is in the east, west, north, or south; whether in a car, airplane, or train- in any place he happens to be, and from any direction or way that he may be able to invite and call to Allaah. He should not lose heart and say, [This is something for someone else to undertake.] Nor should he say, [The people do not have any good in them and they will not accept from me.] No! All of these are statements that should not be said. All of these statements are only pleasing to Shaytaan. Rather what is correct is to speak and pronounce

---

[2]   Narrated in Sunan Ibn Maajah: 4007/ & Musnad Imaam Ahmad: 10862, 11048, 11302, 11458/ -on the authority of Abu Sa'eed al-Khudree. It was declared weak by Sheikh al-Albaanee in Dha'eef at-Targheeb at-Tarheeb: 1387, and in Dha'eef Ibn Maajah. Sheikh Muqbil declared this specific narration to be weak due to having a hidden defect in 'Ahadeeth Mu'alat Dhaaheruha as-Sehah' 155

the truth, and act in accordance to the statement of the One free from all defects: *Invite (mankind, Oh Muhammad) to the Way of your Lord (i.e. Islaam) with wisdom (i.e. with the Divine Inspiration and the Qur'aan) and fair preaching, and argue with them in a way that is better.*-(Surah an-Nahl:125) The "hikmah" mentioned here is knowledge, meaning "*Allaah said*" and "*the Messenger said*". Allaah has designated or referred to knowledge as "hikmah" because it keeps them and holds them within the proper limits; every word that admonishes, reminds, and draws you away from misguidance and calls you towards the truth contains "hikmah" wisdom.

Then following this is admonition and preaching, as some of the hearts are hard and unyielding and require admonishment. There are hearts which will simply not accept and be guided by knowledge alone. If they hear knowledge, they also require admonition until the hearts are softened and accept the truth and are reminded of Allaah, and of the next life, of Paradise in the Hellfire, that this life is by nature transient and passing away ceasing to be anything of worth, that it is not the place which one remains in and invests in. The place one truly will remain is the one which is ahead of you- either Paradise or the Hellfire. So it is necessary to inspire the desire for the rewards that are waiting with Allaah, and a forewarning of the punishment waiting with Allaah, for the one who remains within the boundaries of Allaah's single path or for the one who calls or invites to anything other than that. Due to this, the Most High, Most Exalted, says, *And who is better in speech than he who invites to Allaah, and does righteous deeds, and says: "I am one of the Muslims."*-(Surah Fussilat:33)

So you, oh servant of Allaah, are responsible according to your capacity and condition. The leading scholar, and the student of knowledge, and the discerning common believer in Islaam who understands what is possible in terms of calling to the path of Allaah, and defending the religion with knowledge- all of us have upon us a portion of this responsibility, and upon each of us is the carrying that part of the obligation which we are capable of. This is done along with studying the truth, along with good manners and behavior which leads to reaching the hearts of those who have not been driven away, along with good dealings and dialogue in the best way through which Allaah gives guidance. This is the way which conveys the truth to the hearts. Knowledge is "*Allaah said*" and His "*Messenger said*", and explanation and clarification of this with good speech, good behavior, and good admonishment, as well as to contend with doubts by discussion in the best manner. If doubts and misconceptions arise then seek to benefit by dispersing or dispelling them and desire to preserve the truth by repelling them; then discuss the matter in the best manner until the truth is made clear to those listening, until the misconceptions are removed and Allaah guides them through that the one whom He had determined would be of the people of success and contentment. The paths and ways available today are different than the ones of yesterday. The paths and ways present today are the numerous means and methods of calling to Allaah which are common and which are generally accepted by the people. Therefore it is obligatory upon the people of knowledge and faith in Allaah to develop them upon goodness and to utilize them for the truth and to oppose misguidance, even monetarily, through spending your money freely towards this. There are newspapers outside Saudi Arabia that are only published for the sake of generating money; but here it is possible, and all praise is due to Allaah, to publish and distribute without the extensive lengths or difficulties that they must go through elsewhere. Such a newspaper may be based in a land that requires considerable money to operate, whereas here if a well-known newspaper requires money we ensure that it receives the funds which are the cause of spreading the truth and inviting to it.

Similarly, publishing requires money, as does translating from one language to another language. All these endeavors require tremendous efforts in the path of Allaah, until the truth is spread and invited to according to the degree of your proficiency in the language you understand, as well your ability to spend your financial resources towards producing translations for other people in those languages you wish. Newspapers also must be given priority, as well is publishing and television. They are present amongst us and used by other people even more than us, so it is necessary that attention be directed towards them. It is necessary that scholars as well as the presenters and broadcasters have concern for this, and examine the errors that are found in our newspapers, as well as that which is stated in various publications which is incorrect, and that they explain and clarify these mistakes.

No one should say, [This is for so-and-so to do.] This is a mistake, as it is upon those amongst the scholars and writers who have the ability collectively to contribute to this effort, and to oppose and combat this assault which has been advanced by the enemies of Allaah and their allies. So it is not for anyone to say, [This is not upon for me], because the one who says that should know that every Muslim has a part of obligation. ❴*Oh you who believe! If you help in the cause of Allaah, He will help you, and make your foothold firm.*❵- (Surah Muhammad:7) ❴*And who is better in speech than he who invites men to Allaah, and does righteous deeds.*❵-(Surah Fussilat:33) ❴*This is my way; I invite to Allaah upon insight*❵- (Surah Yusuf:108). ❴*Indeed in the Messenger of Allaah you have a good example to follow*❵-(Surah al-Ahzab:21). Every one of us has upon us an obligation; every Muslim upon Allaah's earth whether in the East or the West, in every area of the world. Every Muslim, every student of knowledge, and every scholar has upon him an obligation to invite to Allaah's religion, that religion which Allaah has ennobled and honored him by, and repelled doubts from him by, and preserved him from conflicts and misguidance by means of behaviors and paths which are known to be beneficial and lead to the truth, and which encourage the acceptance of the truth and which are known to hold back and prevent falsehood and misguidance.

Indeed from the most significant of trials is when an individual says, [I am not responsible for this.]. This is an error and a mistake; a tremendous, false statement which would not be said by someone of intelligence except in the situation where another has satisfied the need amply or completely, where evil has been removed completely by someone else, or the falsehood has been sufficiently opposed by another. In regard to confronting the opponents of Islaam, then this is accomplished by spreading beneficial statements, and offering beneficial essays to oppose what is being published and televised, and to publish that which brings about benefit in the newspapers. Everyone carries a degree of responsibility until truth is given victory, and until falsehood is repelled and suppressed, and until the proof is established against the opponents of Islaam.

The people of misguidance are now supporting each other. The Communists, Christians, and those astray from the remaining groups of misguidance; all of them stand united in purpose against the truth, while they spend their resources freely while they are upon misguidance and callers to the hellfire. Even to the extent that they travel to remote, dangerous locations in their efforts to invite people to the hellfire! Only inviting to the fire! This is seen from the Communists, the Christians, Qadianees, Bahai's and other people of the hellfire or callers to falsehood. The Raafidhah at this time spread their call towards falsehood in every location, in fact slandering the religion of Allaah in that which they are doing in spreading misguidance. They curse the companions of the Prophet, may Allaah's praise and salutations be upon him, and wrongly accuse the Companions of the Prophet, may Allaah's praise and salutations be upon him, as well as their exaggeration towards the members of the Prophet's family, such as Alee, Hassan, Hussein, and others. All of this is from the forms of misguidance, and it prevents from the true path of Allaah. And this is the way and manner of all of the callers to falsehood and misguidance; all of them are upon this methodology.

The danger and falsehood presented by some of them is clear and readily apparent, such as the Christians, the Jews and those similar to them, and the Communists and those similar to them. However, some of them conceal their reality and nature, such as the Raafidhah and the other known categories of the people of innovation in the religion. For example, the Qaadeeanees, who apparently affiliate themselves with Islaam but falsely claim that their leader and founder, Mirza Ghulam, is the prophet whom revelation was given after Muhammad, upon him be Allaah's praise and salutations; so they call to following him. Similarly, this is the method with the other groups and categories of the people of misguidance. It is an obligation for the people of Islaam from every area of the world to spread the truth in opposition to the falsehood found amongst them. Any place where falsehood is found among them there is an obligation upon the people to circulate the truth and to oppose the falsehood; and that the strength of their confronting falsehood with this guidance be greater than that of the falsehood present, until their land, neighborhood, or tribe becomes cleansed from that misguidance which had spread within it. Undertaking this along with teaching the people the truth, and leading them towards the truth and guidance.

It is required that the efforts to be made by the people of knowledge be divided and apportioned, such that the misguidance that is found in their area is given a portion of their efforts, and the other types or occurrences of misguidance are also given a portion of their efforts. However, they should be stronger and more active in the suppression and removal of the misguidance which is found amongst them in their land, until the Muslim ummah becomes secure from that which they have experienced of evil and falsehood. It is required that the people of the truth be more active than the people of misguidance, and more patient in their efforts. If the people of misguidance are patient to the degree of 100% out of 100%, then it is required that the people of truth be patient to the degree of 400% or 1000%, until they become more active than the people of falsehood. Indeed, the people of misguidance only invite to the hellfire while you invite to paradise and true happiness, as well as receiving a greater recompense and reward from our Lord- and the difference between the two is tremendous. Some of the people of misguidance strive with vigor in their false efforts, believing that they are upon the truth and holding that their way is true, while you are also completely secure that you stand upon the truth, all praise is due to Allaah. Allaah, the Most High, says regarding the reality of the people of misguidance, *Surely they took the Shayaateen as protectors and helpers instead of Allaah, and consider that they are guided.*-(Surah al-'Araaf:30) The Christians and those similar to them from the common people believe themselves to be upon guidance, and they are patient and travel to remote areas and unknown lands, inviting to Christianity and so to the Hellfire. They do all this while believing themselves to be guided. Similarly, those who have gone astray from within the Muslims, from the Sufis and other categories of groups which innovate in the religion- the majority of them suppose themselves to be upon guidance; but from their callers and leaders are those who have other objectives and ends in mind. They know they are upon misguidance; however they choose to work towards these other goals and ends in this worldly life. It is therefore obligatory upon the people of truth to be more

74

active, stronger, and more patient in their call to adherence to the following of the Book of Allaah and the Sunnah of the Messenger of Allaah, and proceeding upon the methodology of the companions of the Prophet, upon him be Allaah's praise and salutations.

They must also stick closely to the path of Ahlus-Sunnah wa al-Jama'ah by acting upon everything that Allaah has obligated upon them, and abandoning everything that Allaah has forbidden; directing the people to every matter of truth to be held to, and warning them from every matter of misguidance that is found amongst them, until they are properly guided. Indeed the adviser to the people is the one who directs them to the truth, who directs the one who follows innovated matters towards the true Sunnah, saying to him, "*What you're doing is a mistake, rather, you should do such and such. As Allaah has said such and such and the Messenger, upon him be Allaah's praise and salutations, has said such and such.*" It should be the same way with all the other people of innovation, calling them and directing them towards the truth, hoping that Allaah may guide them from the other ranks of the innovators due to this. And within this month, the month of Rabe' al-Awwal there is an innovation that is widespread in many Muslim lands due to the lack of efforts by the people of knowledge to combat it. That is the innovation of celebrating the Prophet's birthday, may Allaah's praise and salutations be upon him. Additionally, in other lands there are other individual birthdays that are highly esteemed and considered momentous, which the people also celebrate. In these other celebrations there occurs the associating of others with Allaah, aspects of disbelief, and clear misguidance, to a level that only Allaah knows. Similarly in the practices of celebrating the birthday of the Prophet, there occurs from some of its participants associating others with Allaah, and seeking assistance through the Messenger, may Allaah's praise and salutations be upon him, and making supplication to him instead of Allaah, and resorting to that which is the major act of associating of partners with Allaah. And we seek refuge in Allaah from that. This is in addition to what is found within these practices from innovation in the religion, as these celebrations of the Prophets' birthday are a practice which the people invented after the passing of the best generations. Surely, the people before that did not know or practice this innovation of the Prophet's birthday, nor did they in the time of the Prophet, may Allaah's praise and salutations be upon him, nor during the era of his Companions, nor in the age of those Successors to the Companions, and neither was it found in the first second, or third century of Islaam! But it began to be practiced from the fourth century onward, due to the second of the Raafidhah, and those who were ignorant from the people of the Sunnah followed them in that.

It is an obligation upon all of the Muslims to have concern for and to strive to gain understanding of the religion of Allaah, and to gain insight into it, and to seek answers from the people of knowledge regarding their problems and dilemmas; to strive to become close to the Qur'aan and the authentic Sunnah, in order that the student of knowledge understand his religion and stand upon clarity. Also, so that he may be able to convey the correct understanding of the religion to the people found within his community from the general people of his land, region, or from the desert people belonging to his tribe. As information is presently widespread by means of the various forms of media which are being successfully used to spread the truth, just as various statements are spread within the newspapers of this land and others. Similarly, what is being spread by means of publishing the Qur'aan in this land, and what is spread by means of programs (such as radio program "*Light upon the Path*"). Knowledge is being spread through them, and Allaah has benefited many people through these programs and publications, such as the publications of the Qur'aan, as well is in the statements and writings produced by the scholars of many different lands from Egypt, Sham (the region directly north of Saudi Arabia), the lands of the West- Europe and America.

There are, and all praise is due to Allaah, a group of the people of truth spreading the truth in many places. Some of them are doing that by simply distributing flyers or pamphlets. This is a small effort when compared to those of the enemies of Allaah, and yet Allaah has benefited the people through that. What is imperative is that we increase upon these good efforts. That from the people of knowledge and discernment the one who is not speaking, speaks; and the one who is not writing, writes. And even just doing this is not sufficient for them; they must struggle just as those they oppose struggle and they should produce writings just as their enemies do. They must also closely follow the misguidance that is published in circulars, magazines, various types of publications, televisions, and other formats which are used for publication and circulation of material. They must follow and keep track of them and refute the misguidance found within them, spread the truth, and be patient with the difficulties of that, and the hardships of accomplishing that. This is jihaad. This certainly is jihaad. Calling to Allaah is jihaad, and writing in the path of Allaah is jihaad, and altering works for this is also jihaad.

The Prophet, may Allaah's praise and salutations be upon him, said, *{Strive against those who associate others with Allaah with your wealth, your own selves, and your tongues.}* [3]. So calling to Allaah is jihaad. Hassan Ibn Thaabit was a poet of the Messenger, may Allaah's praise and salutations be

---

[3] Narrated in Sunan Abu Daawud: 2156/ Sunan al-Daaramee: 2393/ Mustradraak al-Haakim: 2365/ Sunan an-Nasaa'ee: 4173/ & Musnad Imaam Ahmad: 12029, 13398: -on the authority of 'Anas Ibn Maalik. It was declared authentic by Sheikh al-Albaanee in Saheeh al-Jaame'a as-Sagheer: 3090, Mishkaat al-Masaabeh: 3821, Saheeh Sunan Abu Dawud: 2504, Saheeh Sunan an-Nasaa'ee: 3096.

upon him, and he used to combat against those associated others with Allaah from Mecca with his poetry. The Prophet, may Allaah's praise and salutations be upon him, said to him, *{Strike against them, by the one who has my soul in his hand, as these words against them are harder that arrows descending upon them.}* [4]. And he, upon him be Allaah's praise and salutations, said, *{Strike against them, as certainly the holy spirit (Jibreel) is with you.}* [5]. Meaning by this the angel Jibreel, upon him be Allaah's praise and salutations. So strive against those who associate others with Allaah by writing and poetry which confirms the truth, and statements in publications, and in sermons. All of these are means by which Allaah gives victory to the truth. Additionally the Messenger of Allaah, may Allaah's praise and salutations be upon him, spent the majority of the effort of his call giving sermons, and through speeches. And then by, upon him be Allaah's praise and salutations, writing letters to the leaders and kings of his time. However, the majority of the efforts of his call, upon him be Allaah's praise and salutations, were primarily through sermons and his statements in the city of Medinah and Mecca, yet his other efforts including his military campaigns were also part of his calling to Allaah. All of his endeavors and actions were calling to Allaah, upon him be Allaah's praise and salutations.

Therefore the fundamentals are established by what he did through his actions, his behavior and conduct, his standing and his sitting, his sleeping and his waking. Because of this it is obligatory that the scholars make him

---

[4]   Narrated in Sunan an-Nasaa'ee: 2896/ -on the authority of 'Anas Ibn Maalik. It was declared authentic by Sheikh al-Albaanee in Saheeh Sunan an-Nasaa'ee.

[5]   Narrated in Saheeh al-Bukhaaree: 6153/ Saheeh Muslim: 2486/ & Musnad Imaam Ahmad: 18178, 18203: -on the authority of Bara' Ibn 'Aazab. And it is in Sunan Abu Daawud: 5015/ on the authority of 'Aishah Mother of the Believers. It was declared authentic by Sheikh al-Albaanee in Silsilat al-Hadeeth as-Saheehah: 801, 1970. Saheeh al-Jaame'a as-Sagheer: 3847, 3848, 4287, Saheeh Sunan Abu Dawud, Saheeh Sunan an-Nasaa'ee: 3096. Sheikh Muqbil declared it authentic in al-Jaame'a al-Saheeh: 74, 279, 478, 2563.

the foundation and the basis for establishing and organizing, upon him be Allaah's praise and salutations. However in these latter times Allaah has facilitated this matter for them through these new forms of media which have reached the people in every area and location. These various publications and newspapers which are spread throughout the world can be used to transmit your statements. So if they are based upon the truth Allaah will benefit the people through them, as much as He wills, throughout the entire world. Just as if your words are from falsehood, then many people will be harmed by them. This writing could be done in the city of Riyadh and then reach Europe, America, and every other region, spreading through that original composition to every location. They may be used in various types of publications, or in television and then spread to every place, not merely in its original form or instance. But in the beginning it was a limited publication specifically in your country or within the surrounding region. However, today one makes a statement and in one day or one night, rather in a single hour- you make a statement and it is heard by the whole world, from this land and from that land.

Again, if it was a word of truth then the blessing will come from it, and if it was a word of falsehood than what results from it is only harm and offense. And there is no strength or power except in Allaah. As the people must consider-consider and take into account the condition of the people today. One might give a sermon in America and it is heard by the people everywhere. Someone may give a sermon in Egypt and it is heard by many people, or give one in Mecca and it is heard by many people, or in Riyadh and it is heard by many people as well is being heard in other places- regardless of whether it is for truth or for falsehood.

For the people, whether calling to guidance or to falsehood, are heard by the people. And the majority of the people are not upon guidance, and indeed there is no strength or power except in Allaah. The majority of people are following their desires. *And if you obey most of those on earth, they will mislead you far away from Allaah's Path. They follow nothing but conjectures, and they do nothing but lie*-(Surah al-An'aam 116) *And most of mankind will not believe even if you desire it eagerly.*-(Surah Yusuf:103). So the majority of humanity are upon their misguidance, wishes, and desires, but not upon the truth. The truth can only be brought to light through the people of insight and understanding, the people of sound intellect, the people of investigation, discernment, consideration, and intelligence; those who possess the ability to distinguish between truth and falsehood, those who comprehend the consequences and outcomes of matters upon faith and sound understanding. However, the majority of the humanity are in a state like that which Allaah, the Most High, Most Exalted, mentioned, saying, *Or do you think that most of them hear or understand? They are only like cattle; nay, they are even farther astray from the Path.*-(Surah al-Furqaan: 44) He has declared them to be more astray than cattle, meaning that some animals are more guided than some of humanity, as they benefit the people. They proceed upon their affair of simply grazing and other activities but do not cause harm or difficulty for the people. But as for the majority of humanity, they are more harmful than the animals; they do not benefit, but instead bring harm to people. We ask Allaah for safety and health. And in this there is a lesson for the person of intelligence to take care such that you benefit and do not bring harm, whether seeking to benefit people by your statements, actions, wealth, power or other matters that benefit- not from matters that would bring harm to the people.

From the trials and tribulations is when someone works, believing that he is upon guidance, believing that he is benefiting in bringing good, when reality is harming the people. Just as Allaah says, *Say: "Shall We tell you the greatest losers in respect of (their) deeds? Those whose efforts have been wasted in this life while they thought that they were acquiring good by their deeds!*-(Surah Kahf:103-104) And this is from a tremendous loss; that one strives diligently with their wealth, time, and the various types of efforts, but in that which in reality does not benefit them, but only harms them. It is from the matters that anger Allaah and which prevent the spread of the truth. So certainly it is one of the tremendous losses and we ask Allaah for safety and health. Therefore the person of intelligence brings himself to account and struggles within himself. He considers carefully and is not silent within himself nor heedless. He considers what it is that he endeavoring upon and what he is sending forth for the next world- thinking and considering carefully. Just as the Most Exalted says, *Oh you who believe! Fear Allaah and keep your duty to Him. And let every person look to what he has sent forth for the morrow, and fear Allaah. Verily, Allaah is All-Aware of what you do. And be not like those who forgot Allaah (i.e. became disobedient to Allaah) and He caused them to forget their own selves, (let them to forget to do righteous deeds). Those are the Faasiqun (rebellious, disobedient to Allaah). Not equal are the dwellers of the Fire and the dwellers of the Paradise. It is the dwellers of Paradise that will be successful*-(Surah al-Hashr:18-20)

So the person of intelligence proceeds and looks and considers what he has sent forward, what has he done for the next world, and his next life! What has he put forward which opposes misguidance, what has he undertaken for the success and contentment of his wife, children, neighbor, and society. Do not be heedless! It is required that he continually and constantly questions and considers. Is he in a state of loss or one of profit and success? Is he content or in misery? Is he upon guidance or misguidance? Consider and evaluate yourself all the time, and make yourself adhere to the truth that you understand- hold fast to the truth by preserving your congregational prayer, by paying the zakaat charity, by good treatment to one's parents, by maintaining family ties, by staying away from the different forms of immoral behavior, and by leaving evil companionship. Similarly, calling yourself to account- so the one who drinks intoxicants calls himself to account and abandons those intoxicants completely, the one who sits with people who are bad or evil companions should call himself to account and distance himself from them. Look carefully at your actions; are they benefiting or harming you? Are you working in that which will benefit you in the next life or acting in a way that will lead to Hellfire? Call yourself to account.

This is an incredibly dangerous age where one sees misguidance everywhere. The radio broadcasts are present, television is present, and newspapers are present all containing evil and harm, the true extent of which is only known by Allaah. You listen with your ears, and see with your own eyes, and write with your own pen, or read; so consider what is achieved from all this. What is actually attained from listening to media broadcasts and watching television, or from reading the newspaper? Have you obtained goodness and benefit or only acquired harm and evil? So if you have only reached harm then be warned and stop. But if you have achieved goodness and benefit then all praise is due to Allaah, continue upon that good, being warned from falsehood and misguidance. Then do not stop only with yourself as an individual, advise your brother, your wife, your father and mother, your child, your neighbor and your friend. Advise them if you witness misguidance that will harm them as it would harm you, as the Muslim is the brother of the Muslim. The Messenger of Allaah, upon him be Allaah's praise and salutations, said,

{One of you does not truly believe until he loves for his brother what he loves for himself.} [6]. And he said, may Allaah's praise and salutations be upon him, *{"The religion is sincerity and well wishing." Upon this we said, "For whom?" He replied, "For Allaah, His Book, His Messenger and for the leaders and the general Muslims."}* [7].

If the giving of advice before this age or before these new occurrences and developments was an obligation, then today it is now a much greater obligation. If calling to Allaah a hundred years ago or two hundred years ago was an obligation, then today it is a much greater obligation- and so on. As the situation now is that overwhelming evil, as falsehood has dominated and spread. So it is obligatory to double one's efforts to oppose and combat it. All of these are aspects of this ideological war and warfare which are talked about. And it is that struggle which reaches you by means of the television, newspapers, publications, and other authored works; all of these are part of the ideological war, and the war to cause you to abandon Islaam. It is a very damaging war, that harms everyone except the few who are protected by your Lord's mercy. I ask Allaah by His beautiful names and exalted attributes to bless us and you with beneficial knowledge and righteous deeds, and to grant us understanding of the religion and steadfastness upon it and to protect us from the evil of our own selves and from our own evil deeds. And to bless us with the true jihaad against ourselves and that we call

---

[6]   Narrated in Saheeh al-Bukhaaree: 13/ Saheeh Muslim: 45/ Jaame'a at-Tirmidhee: 2515/ Saheeh Sunan an-Nasaa'ee: 5016, 5017, 5043/ Sunan Ibn Maajah: 66/ & Musnad Imaam Ahmad: 12390, 12734, and other narrations/ Sunan ad-Daaramee: 2740/ -on the authority of 'Anas Ibn Maalik. It was declared authentic by Sheikh al-Albaanee in Silsilat al-Hadeeth as-Saheehah: 73, Mishkaat al-Masaabeeh: 4961, Saheeh al-Jaame'a as-Sagheer: 7085, 7583, as well as in Saheeh Sunan at-Tirmidhee and Saheeh Sunan an-Nasaa'ee.

[7]   Narrated in Saheeh Muslim: 2, 55/ Sunan Abu Daawud: 4933/ Saheeh Sunan an-Nasaa'ee: 4202, 4203/ & Musnad Imaam Ahmad: 16493, 16494, and other narrations/ -on the authority of Tameem ad-Daaree. And it is narrated in Jaame'a at-Tirmidhee: 1926/ Saheeh Sunan an-Nasaa'ee: 4204, 4205/ & Musnad Imaam Ahmad: 7894/ -on the authority of Abu Hurairah It was declared authentic by Sheikh al-Albaanee in Irwa' al-Ghaleel : 26, Mishkaat al-Masaabeeh: 4966, and other of his works.

ourselves into accounting order that we are firm upon the truth, and leave misguidance.

I ask that He bless us and you with excellent companions and righteous associates and that He protect us and all the Muslims from evil companions and harmful associates, and that He grant success to the scholars of the Muslims in every place to spread the truth and establish what is required of them in calling to it, and being patient upon that endeavor. And that He grants success to the Muslim rulers in all parts of the world to be upon a way that He is pleased with. And that He support them in spreading the truth and ruling by the truth, and suppressing falsehood, thus combating falsehood and misguidance and its people wherever they are found. And that He protects them from obeying their desires and Shaytaan, as Allaah, the Most High and Exalted is the Most Giving and the Most Generous.

We ask Him by His noble face to guide our rulers and people of authority to every good, and through them give victory to the truth. And that He assist them in the rectification of these various forms of media and communication until evil and harm are removed from within them and good is firmly established within them, and that they become our tools of goodness and rectification from every aspect and direction, and that Allaah remove from them every harm or tribulation. And that He bless our scholars and the scholars of all the Muslims in every location, to fulfill their obligations and spread the truth, and that He blesses the common Muslims with insight and consideration and steadfastness upon the truth and to be of those who inquire about the truth and abandon misguidance, and to advise with the truth in their various affairs between them. Certainly He is the one who hears and is close to us. And that Allaah's praise and salutations be upon our prophet Muhammad, his family, and his Companions.

Question: You have mentioned in your presentation that it is upon all the students of knowledge to speak and act for Allaah's religion; and this is true may Allaah reward you with good, as this regard neglect has occurred from the direction of the students of knowledge specifically. However there is also an important point to be made, and it is that it is not permissible for them that they speak except after having received permission, otherwise they will be fall into trials and difficulties. As speaking publicly has conditions, which are not fulfilled by every student of knowledge. Due to this it is necessary that they leave this realm to those who possess the necessary characteristics. What is your opinion regarding this?

Answer: Such permission is a simple matter and all praise is due to Allaah, as everyone who is known with good then he is given permission. And we do not give the right to speak to just anyone, such that they might speak and invite towards misguidance and spread falsehood- no. But this matter, all praise is due to Allaah, is simple, as the one who is known to have knowledge or has graduated from the college of Sharee'ah, or from the college of "the fundamentals of the religion", or the scholars testify to goodness regarding him- even if it is a single scholar, then he is given such permission, and he can proceed to speak and give sermons, and all praise is due to Allaah.

['A Lecture Discussing the Ideological War' & the First Question following the Lecture]

85

(8)

QUESTION: SOME OF THOSE WHO CALL TO ALLAAH AVOID UTILIZING VARIOUS TYPES OF MEDIA BECAUSE OF THEIR REJECTION OF ANY GOVERNMENT CONTROLLED NEWSPAPER OR REJECT WORKING A MAGAZINE WHICH GENERALLY RELIES UPON SENSATIONAL ARTICLES TO INCREASE THEIR CIRCULATION AMONG THE PEOPLE. SO WHAT IS YOUR ESTEEMED VIEW REGARDING THIS?

nswer: It is an obligation for those responsible for such newspapers to have fear of Allaah and to guard against those things which harm the people. Regardless of whether this is a daily, weekly, or monthly newspaper. Likewise, the authors should fear Allaah in the material they author. Do not write or publish among the general people except what will benefit them and which invites them to good and warns them against evil. As for the publishing of images of women on the covers of or inside of magazines or newspapers, then this is a tremendous evil, and significant harm, which invites to corruption and misguidance. Similarly, is the publishing of material which call to false socialist ideas or material that invites to sinful behavior, such as adultery, and the exposure of women's beauty outside of proper situations, the using of intoxicants or any matter that Allaah has made forbidden. All of these are tremendous evils, and it is required that those responsible for these periodicals take care to stay away from these matters.

When such things are published they are accountable for the wrongdoing which the people were encouraged towards. As for the responsible individual associated with this periodical which publishes these blameworthy articles, whether he is the editor or an administrator who instructs them with that, he has upon him an equal share of the sins of the people who are misguided by this material and affected by it. Just as the one who publishes that which is good and that which calls to good and beneficial matters receives a reward equal to the one who is affected by it in a good way.

From this starting point, clearly it is obligatory upon the various media organizations which have a tremendous effect and hold upon the Muslims, to ensure that they are free from everything which Allaah has prohibited and that they stay far away from spreading that which undoubtedly harms the society.

In view of this, is it an obligation upon these various organizations to make their primary focus and goal that which benefits the people in regard to their religion and worldly affairs. And that they guard against becoming instruments for the destruction of society and the means for its corruption by means of what they publish. Each responsible individual in such a media organization is responsible for this to the degree of his capacity and ability.

And it is an obligation upon the callers that they utilize the opportunities offered by the media to warn against all matters forbidden by Allaah the Most High, the Most Exalted. This is an obligation upon them in their sermons and their gatherings with the people. Every sitting should be a gathering of invitation to good wherever it is. As he is calling to Allaah whether it is within his house, when visiting brothers, or when he gathers or meets with anyone. As it is required from him that he utilize these ways and means, meaning the various forms of media, and spread good through them and not neglect making proper use of them..

[FROM ' 'A COLLECTION OF RULINGS AND VARIOUS STATEMENTS': VOL.5, PAGE 266]

(9)

QUESTION: CLEARLY, BRINGING GUIDANCE TO THE PEOPLE IS THE RESULT OF SPREADING SHAREE'AH KNOWLEDGE AMONG THEM, HOWEVER WE SEE THAT FALSEHOOD IS MORE WIDELY SPREAD OVER MOST NEWSPAPERS AND THE VARIOUS TYPES OF MEDIA, AS WELL AS WITHIN THE EDUCATION METHODOLOGIES AND CURRICULUMS. SO WHAT IS THE POSITION OF THE SCHOLAR AND THE CALLER TO ALLAAH REGARDING THIS?

nswer: This reality is something found in every age and the wisdom of this is something Allaah willed just as He states: ❊ *And most of the people will not believe even if you desire it eagerly* ❊-(Surah Yusuf:103) and the Most Exalted says: ❊ *And if you obey most of those on earth, they will mislead you far away from Allaah's Path* ❊-(Surah al-Ana'am:116) However this differs, as in one land it will be greater in degree and in another less, and in one tribe it may be greater and in another less. But in regard to the world in general, then the majority of people are upon something other than guidance- yet this varies for some of the countries, lands, regions, and tribes.

Therefore, it is obligatory upon the people of knowledge to strive vigorously and not let the people of falsehood out strive them. Rather, it is obligatory that they out strive the people of falsehood in their efforts to make the truth clear -calling to it wherever they may be, whether in the street, in a car, in an airplane, in a spaceship, in his home, in any location. It is for them to prevent wrongdoing in the way that is best, and carry this out in the best manner with excellent behavior, gentleness and mildness.

As the Most High and the Most Exalted says: "Invite to the Way of your Lord with wisdom and fair preaching, and argue with them in a way that is better." (Surah an-Nahl: 125) And the One free from all faults says: ❊ *And by the Mercy of Allaah, you dealt with them gently. And had you been severe and harsh hearted, they would have broken away from about you* ❊-(Surah Aal-'Imraan:159) And the Prophet, may Allah's praise and salutations be upon him, said: *{The one who guides to goodness received a reward equal to the who does it..}*-(Saheeh Muslim: 1893) He, prayers and salutations be upon him, said: *{Gentleness in not found with a matter except that it beautifies it and it is not absent from a matter except that this absence tarnishes or taints it.}*-(Saheeh Muslim: 2594)

So it is not permissible for the people of knowledge to remain silent and abandon speaking to the sinner, the innovator, and the ignorant one. As this is a tremendous mistake and from the causes of the spread of evil and innovation, the removal of goodness and it being something scarce and the disappearance of the Sunnah.

It is obligatory upon the people of knowledge to speak with the truth and invite towards it and to censure falsehood and warn away from it. And it is obligatory to do this with upon knowledge and insight, as Allaah the Most High, the Most Exalted says: ﴾ *This is my way; I invite unto Allah with sure knowledge*﴿-(Surah Yusuf:108). And this is after attention being given the means by which knowledge is acquired through studying with the people of knowledge, and asking them regarding ones problems, attending their circles of knowledge, frequently reciting the Noble Qur'aan, contemplating it and reviewing authentic narrations.

This until one benefits and knowledge spreads forth by way of it being taken from its people with evidence with sincerity, a good intention, and humility. It obligatory for them to be diligent in the spreading of knowledge with every vigor and strength, and to not allow the people of falsehood to be more active than them in the spreading of their falsehood, being diligent to benefit the Muslims in their religious and worldly affairs. So this is an obligation upon the scholars, the elders and the young among them wherever they may be, to spread the truth through its Sharee'ah evidences and encourage the people towards it, and turn them away from falsehood and warn them from it in practice, as Allaah the Most High, and The Most Exalted says: ﴾ *Cooperate with one another upon goodness and the fear of Allah*﴿-(Surah al-Maidah:2)

And the statement of the Most High: ❧ *By al-'Asr (the time). Verily! Man is in loss. Except those who believe and do righteous good deeds, and recommend one another to the truth, and recommend one another to patience.* ❧-(Surah al-Asr:1-3)

Likewise, the people of knowledge wherever they are should call to Allah- guiding towards goodness, giving advice to Allaah and His worshipers, with gentleness in that which they command towards, that which the forbid from, and that which they call to -until their call becomes successful and the majority of the people realize a praiseworthy effect and are protected from the plots of our enemies. And from Allaah we seek assistance

[*'A COLLECTION OF RULINGS AND VARIOUS STATEMENTS': VOL. 9, PAGE 223]*

(10)

QUESTION: THE YOUTH INVOLVED IN THE REVIVAL OF ISLAAM ARE COMMONLY ACCUSED OF EXTREMISM AND "FUNDAMENTALISM" IN SOME OF THE VARIOUS MEDIA SOURCES. WHAT IS YOUR ESTEEMED VIEW OF THIS?

nswer: Regardless of this, this is a error which originates from the Western countries from the Christians and Jews, and from the Eastern countries from the communists as well as other than them, from those who want to turn others away from the call to Allaah and those who support it. They wish to stain and slander this call by such accusations or by using the label of "fundamentalism" or this or that term which they label them with. There is no doubt that calling to Allaah is the religion of all the Prophets of Allaah; this was their way and their path. It is obligatory upon the people of knowledge to invite to Allaah and to do this vigorously. Additionally it is upon those young men who fear and have reverence of Allaah, and who hold fast to the truth, that they do not go towards extremism nor negligence.

As some of the young men are ignorant and so the act with extremism in some matters, while others have a deficiency in knowledge and so they are ignorant of their religion. However, it is upon all of the young men as well as others such as the scholars that they fear Allaah and that they investigate and search for the truth of matters by their evidences, by this meaning: "*Allaah, the Most High, the Most Exalted says*", and "*the Messenger of Allaah, may Allaah's praise and salutations be upon him, says*". It is also upon them to stay far away from innovation in the religion and extremism and going beyond the proper limits. As well as also staying far away from ignorance and deficiencies in their practice. There is no one among them who is infallible, so there has occurred from some of the people matters of deficiency in the religion, either by adding something or falling short in something. However this is not something all of them can be faulted with, it is only a fault in the specific one from whom it occurs.

The enemies of Allaah from the Christians and others who are upon their same path, use this as a means to strike at and attack the call to Allaah. As well as to cast upon the Muslims the accusation that they are "extremists" or "fundamentalists". And what is the meaning of the term "fundamentalist"? If they are fundamentalist meaning that: that hold firm to the fundamentals of Islaam, and to what Allaah has stated and what the Messenger of Allaah, prayers and good mention be upon him, has stated- then this is in praise of them not censure. Being described with adherence to the Book of Allaah and the Sunnah of the Messenger of Allaah, prayers and good mention be upon him, is certainly praise and is not truly criticism. Rather what is worthy of censure is going to extremes or laxity either through acting in an extreme way by going beyond the proper bounds, or by going to the other extreme through neglect and falling short of what is required. This is what is to be criticized.

As for the individual who holds firmly to the recognized foundations and principles from the Book of Allaah and the Sunnah of His Messenger, prayers and good mention be upon him, then this is not at all blameworthy. Rather it is praiseworthy and from te completion of the religion. This is what is required upon the students of knowledge and the callers to Allaah: that they hold firmly to the foundations from the Book of Allaah and the Sunnah of His Messenger, prayers and good mention be upon him, and what they understand from the principles of deriving the rules of the religion, and the fundamentals of correct belief, and fundamentals of hadeeth terminology in regard to what is used in determining the status of what is accepted as evidence. It is necessary that that they have the understanding of these fundamentals as a foundation that must be relied upon.

So they attack the callers to Allaah with the accusation that they are "fundamentalists", and this statement is intentionally broad without having a corresponding reality, except to throw blame, find fault, and cause fear. As such this label of so called "fundamentalism" is not blameworthy, but in reality is a commendation and statement of praise. If a student of knowledge holds firmly to the fundamentals, has true concern for them, and attends to them carefully- and what is intended by fundamentals is what comes from the Book of Allaah and the Sunnah of His Messenger, prayers and good mention be upon him, and from what has been established by the people of knowledge- then this is not at all blameworthy. But as for going to extremes by innovating matters in the religion, and making additions, and extremism, then this is indeed blameworthy. Or the going to extremes through ignorance and neglect, that is also blameworthy.

It is obligatory upon the callers to adhere to the fundamentals of the Sharee'ah and to hold firmly to them with the moderation that Allaah placed them upon. As Allaah has made the Muslim nation a balanced moderate nation. So it is obligatory upon the callers to: to be moderate between immoderation and inattention, between excess and negligence. And it is upon them to be established upon the truth, and to affirm this by Sharee'ah evidences. Not by excess and extremism, and not by inattention nor negligence. Rather, with the moderation and balance which Allaah has commanded.

[FROM 'COLLECTION OF RULINGS AND VARIOUS STATEMENTS': VOL. 8 - PAGE 232-234]

(11)

QUESTION: IT IS WELL KNOWN HOW MUCH GOOD THE ISLAMIC RECORDING DISTRIBUTORS HAVE ACCOMPLISHED IN THE PRESENT TIME AND THEIR IMPORTANT ROLE IN GUIDING THE PEOPLE. HOWEVER SOME PEOPLE OF EVIL INTENT ATTEMPT TO DISTORT THE REPUTATION AND STATE THAT THEY ARE ONLY ENGAGED IN MAKING MONEY AND OTHER STATEMENTS THAT MALIGN THEM. I HOPE THAT, ESTEEMED SHEIKH, YOUR WOULD CLARIFY THIS IMPORTANT ISSUE FOR THE PEOPLE, TO PROTECT THEM FROM THE DECEPTIONS OF THE ONES WHO DON'T HAVE INSIGHT INTO MATTERS.

nswer: There is no doubt that the attention given to recording beneficial statements, and sermons, and beneficial speeches. All of this benefits the Muslim nation, and the one who has done so for the benefit of the Ummah then he is thanked. And he should hold to patience and hope for Allaah's reward for those efforts. Even if evil is said about him then he is following the example of Allaah's messengers, may Allaah's praise and salutations be upon them, as well as those excellent predecessors who come before him. So there is no harm in selling audio cassettes of these types of speech, at a affordable price which will not cause difficulty for the people. He can use this money to assist him in his work while benefiting the people by spreading knowledge, and making beneficial material widely available. I advise you to acquire good tapes, and I recommend that the people purchase and benefit from them, if they are beneficial and upright tapes. Yet not every audio cassette is beneficial and upright, and not every speaker is one who truly produces beneficial speech which is actually worthy of recording. Therefore it is obligatory upon the student of knowledge to select audio cassettes which originate from the people of knowledge well known for realizing knowledge, and then benefit from them. He should also play them for his family, his brothers, and friends. And to stay away from those recordings that which will not benefit him or which may harm him

[FROM 'COLLECTION OF RULINGS AND VARIOUS STATEMENTS':]

(12)

QUESTION: THE STATEMENT HAS SPREAD AMONG THE STUDENTS OF KNOWLEDGE ESPECIALLY IN THE COLLEGES AND INSTITUTIONS OF KNOWLEDGE THAT: [KNOWLEDGE HAS LEFT WITH THE PASSING OF THE PEOPLE OF KNOWLEDGE, AND THOSE WHO NOW STUDY IN THE INSTITUTIONS OF KNOWLEDGE DO SO ONLY FOR THE PURPOSE OF OBTAINING DEGREES OR THE BENEFITTING IN THIS WORLD]. SO WHAT IS THE RESPONSE TO THEM? ADDITIONALLY, WHAT IS THE RULING OF COMBINING THE INTENTION FOR A WORLDLY BENEFIT OR RECEIVING A DIPLOMA ALONG WITH ONE'S INTENTION TO SEEK KNOWLEDGE TO BENEFIT ONESELF AND ONE'S SOCIETY?

nswer: This speech is not correct, and it is not proper to make this statement or statements similar to it. The one who says [the people are destroyed], rather he he is the most ruined among them! However encouragement and motivation towards the seeking of knowledge is what is required, devotion to it, having patience and persevering upon it, having the good suspicion of the students of knowledge, except for the one you know who clearly differs from this. And when death came to Mua'dh Ibn Jabal it is said that he advised his students of knowledge around him saying: *"For the one who truly wants them, certainly knowledge and faith are here and available."* meaning: Their location being the Book of Allaah the Mighty, and the Sunnah of His trustworthy Messenger, may Allaah's praise and salutations be upon him.

The scholar is taken with his knowledge and so knowledge is removed through the death of the scholars, however all praise is due to Allaah, there will never cease to be a group victories upon the truth. Due to this the Messenger, upon him be Allaah's praise and salutations, said: *{Verily, Allaah does not take away knowledge by plucking it from the chests of the people but He takes away knowledge by the passing away of the scholars, so that when there is no scholar present, the people turn to the ignorant as their leaders; then they are asked to deliver religious verdicts and so they deliver them without knowledge, they go astray, and lead others astray.}* [1]. This is what one should be afraid of, being wrongly put forwards to give Islamic rulings and therefor teaching ignorance, such that you are from those who are astray and are sending other astray.

---

[1] Narrated in Saheeh al-Bukhaaree: 100, 7307/ Saheeh Muslim: 4829 / Sunan at-Tirmidhee: 2576/ Sunan Ibn Maajah: 51/ Musnad Of Ahmad: 6222, 6498, 6602/ & Sunan ad-Daaramee: 239 from the hadeeth of 'Abdullah Ibn 'Umar Ibn al-'Aas.

As for the statement which is made: [Knowledge has left. There is nothing left except for such and such] One should fear from making this statement due to possibly leading of some of the people towards being discouraged. But if one if steadfast and has insight one should not be discouraged from this statement. Rather, it should push you towards seeking knowledge, until that clear need of the Muslims is fulfilled. Additionally the sincere person of understanding, and the truthful person of insight are not disheartened by the likes of this statement. Rather, they step forward and take the initiative to strive hard, persevere, study, and move quickly due to the intense demand for knowledge, and to fulfill that need which is claimed by those who make this statement: [No one remains...] But what has actually occurred is that there is a clear deficiency of knowledge as well as the passing away of it people.

However, all praise is due to Allaah, there has not ceased to be a group upon the victorious truth. Just as the Prophet, may Allaah's praise and salutations be upon him, said: *{There will not cease to be a group from my Ummah victorious upon the truth. They are not harmed by those who oppose them nor by those that leave them, until Allaah's command or judgment comes.}* [2]

It is upon us to strive in seeking knowledge, and to encourage others towards it, and be diligent regarding the significant need for it, and establishing its obligation in our land as well as others, acting upon the Sharee'ah evidences in this, desiring the benefiting and teaching of the Muslims.

---

[2] Narrated in Saheeh al-Bukhaaree: 3641, 7460/ Saheeh Muslim: 1037/ & Musnad Imaam Ahmad: 16485/-on the authority of Mu'aweeyah. And it was narrated in Saheeh Muslim: 1920/ & Musnad Imaam Ahmad: 21897/-on the authority of Thawbaan Ibn Bujaddid. And it was narrated in Jaame'a at-Tirmidhee: 2192/ Sunan Ibn Maajah: 6/ & Musnad Imaam Ahmad: 19849/ - -from the hadeeth of Qurrat Ibn Eyaas. It was declared authentic by Sheikh al-Albaanee in Silsilat al-Hadeeth as-Saheehah: 1957, and Sheikh Muqbil declared it authentic in al-Jaame'a al-Saheeh: 2384.

Also it is required that we should encourage others towards purity of intention and truthfulness in the seeking of knowledge. The one who desires a diploma, to strengthen his efforts to convey knowledge and call to goodness, then he does well in that. And the one who desires money in order to be strengthen by it - there is no harm if he studies, learns and obtains a diploma which will assist in the spreading knowledge, and by which the people will then accept from him this knowledge, and to take money that will assist him in that effort. As if it were it not for Allaah, glorified is He and then wealth, many people would not be able to call and invite and convey this call. So wealth helps the Muslim upon seeking knowledge, and upon fulfilling his needs, and conveying knowledge to the people.

As when Umar, may Allaah be pleased with him did some work for the Messenger of Allaah, may Allaah's praise and salutations be upon him, gave him some money. But 'Umar said *"Give it to someone poorer than me."* So the Prophet, may Allaah's praise and salutations be upon him, said: *{Take this wealth to increase what you have or give it in charity. That which comes to you from this wealth without your hoping for it nor without begging- take it, but in other circumstance's do not let yourself pursue or run after it.}* It is narrated by Imaam Muslim in his 'Saheeh' collection. The Prophet, may Allaah's praise and salutations be upon him, gave to some of them to unite their hearts, and encourage them such that they would enter into Allaah's religion in numbers. If it was prohibited he would not have given to them, and in reality he distributed wealth to them before and after the conquest of Mecca. And during the Day of Conquest of Mecca, he gave to some people one hundred camels, and he gave gifts to those whom he did not fear poverty for them, upon him be Allaah's praise and salutations, encouraging them towards Islaam and calling them towards it.

Allaah, free from any imperfection has decreed that a portion from Zakaat be given for those who hearts would be be united through It. He decreed that from what was in the public treasury they had portion and others such as teachers and judges had a portion, as did other from among the Muslims. And Allaah is the Best Guardian and the source of success.

[FROM "COLLECTION OF RULINGS AND VARIOUS STATEMENTS": VOL. 7 PAGE 231]

(13)

QUESTION: WHAT DO YOU SAY

REGARDING WOMEN

& CALLING ALLAAH?

nswer: In relation to this she is similar to the man in that she should call to Allaah, enjoin everything good, and forbid wrongdoing. This is because the source texts of the Noble Qur'aan, and the pure Sunnah generally indicate this, and the statements of the people of knowledge directly state this. Therefore, she should call to Allaah, enjoin everything good, and forbid wrongdoing using the proper Islamic manners and etiquette, which are also desired from men. Along with this she should not allow herself to become discouraged from calling to Allaah due to hastiness or a lack of patience, nor by the contempt and disdain that some of the people have towards her or their speaking against her or mocking her. No. Rather, she should endure this and have patience, even if she see a kind of jeering and mockery from the people. In addition to this, it is upon her to consider and look at another matter, and this is that she should be a model of modesty and should shield herself from foreign men outside of her family, and distance herself from free mixing. Indeed, her endeavors of calling must be put forth along with diligent attention to preserving herself from every matter that they may pour blame upon her concerning. If she calls a man to what is correct then she calls him while she is properly wearing hijaab and without being secluded with any foreign man. When she calls and invites women she does so with wisdom and insight. She should be upright in her character and lifestyle so that they do not turn away from her, and do not say "*Why doesn't she begin with correcting herself!*" It is also upon her to stay away from wearing any type of clothes that which cause trials or problems among the people, and to be far away from every cause of strife and trials, from displaying aspects of her beauty or unwarranted softness in her speech, which are from those matters that she might be considered blameworthy for. Rather, she should be diligent in calling to Allaah in a manner that does not harm her practice of the religion nor harm her reputation

[A COLLECTION OF RULINGS AND VARIOUS STATEMENTS':
VOL. 4, PAGE 240]

(14)

QUESTION: I HAVE LEFT MY STUDIES AND
MY MOTHER IS NOT PLEASED WITH THIS.
AM I A WRONGDOER DUE TO THIS?

nswer: Studying and learning contain tremendous good and significant benefits, and it is obligatory upon each Muslim man and woman to learn and understand the religion. It is required upon every Muslim to understand his religion and learn those matters in which ignorance cannot be accepted. From the causes of contentment and happiness is gaining an understanding of the religion. The Prophet, may Allaah praise and salutations be upon said, *{Whoever Allaah intends good for He grants him understanding in the religion.}* [1]. As such, from the signs of being granted contentment and satisfaction is having an understanding of Allaah's religion, and gaining understanding of the Sharee'ah such that a Muslim then understands what is obligatory upon him, and what is forbidden for him, and such that he worships Allaah upon understanding and insight. This is found in the statement of the Prophet, may Allaah praise and salutations be upon him, *{Whoever goes forth upon the path of seeking knowledge, Allaah makes easy for him the path to Jannah.}* [2]

Therefore it is obligatory upon you that you learn and gain understanding of the religion if that is facilitated for you in a good trustworthy Islamic school. Especially if your mother is encouraging and pushing you towards this, then that is something which just makes it more obligatory that you be concerned and diligent in gaining an understanding of your religion.

[1]   Narrated in Saheeh al-Bukhaaree: 71, 3116, 7312/ Saheeh Muslim: 1037/ Sunan Ibn Maajah: 221/ al-Muwatta Maalik: 1300, 1667/ Musnad Imaam Ahmad: 16395: 16404, and other narrations/ Musannaf Ibn Abee Shaybah: 31792/ & Sunan ad-Daaramee: 224, 226/- on the authority of Mu'aweeyah. And it is found in Jaame'a al-Tirmidhee: 2645/ & Musnad Imaam Ahmad: 2786/ & Sunan ad-Daaramee: 270, 2706/- on the authority of Ibn "Abbaas. And it is found in Sunan Ibn Maajah: 220/ Musannaf 'Abdul-Razzaaq: 30851/- on the authority of Abu Hurairah. It was declared authentic by Sheikh al-Albaanee in Saheeh al-Aadab al-Mufrad: 517, Silsilat al-Hadeeth as-Saheehah: 1194, 1195, 1196, Saheeh at-Targheeb at-Tarheeb: 67, as well as in other of his books. Sheikh Muqbil declared it authentic in al-Jaame'a al-Saheeh: 9, 3123, 4650.

[2]   Narrated in Saheeh Muslim: 2699/ Sunan at-Tirmidhee: 2945/ Sunan Ibn Maajah: 225 / & Musnad Ahmad: 7379- from the hadeeth of Abu Hurairah. Declared authentic by Sheikh al-Albaanee in Saheeh at-Targheeb wa al-Tarheeb: 69, 89, as well as in other of his books.

She only wants good for you, and your true benefit in this world as well as the next. So it is not proper that you disobey her in this request except if the specific school is one that mixes the students of both genders together or which has some other characteristics which may harm your religion. In that case there is no harm in your leaving studying in that place even if your mother is not pleased with this, because the Messenger of Allaah, may Allaah's praise and salutations be upon him, said, *{Verily, obedience is only in that which is good and permissible.}* [3]. And he said *{There is no obedience to the creation in that which is disobedience to the Creator}* [4].

[FROM 'COLLECTION OF RULINGS AND VARIOUS STATEMENTS' VOL.9, PAGE 337 & VOL. 8, PAGE 317]

---

[3]   Narrated in Saheeh al-Bukhaaree: 7145, 7257/ Saheeh Muslim: 1840/ Sunan Abu Dawud: 2625/Sunan an-Nasaa'ee: 4210/ Musnad Imaam Ahmad: 623, 723, 1021/ -on the authority of 'Alee Ibn Abee Taalib. It was declared authentic by Sheikh al-Albaanee in Silsilat al-Hadeeth as-Saheehah: 181, Mishkaat al-Masaabeh: 3665, & Saheeh al-Jaame'a as-Sagheer: 7319, 7519, and in his verification of al-'Emaan by Ibn Taymeeyah.

[4]   Narrated in Musnad Imaam Ahmad: 1098/ -on the authority of 'Alee Ibn Abee Taalib. It was declared authentic by Sheikh al-Albaanee in Silsilat al-Hadeeth as-Saheehah: 179, Mishkaat al-Masaabeh: 3696, & Saheeh al-Jaame'a as-Sagheer: 7520.

(15)

QUESTION: WE FIND THAT SOME OF THE COMMON PEOPLE AND THE STUDENTS OF KNOWLEDGE MAKE STATEMENTS REGARDING SHAREE'AH ISSUES, WHILE NOT BEING FROM THE PEOPLE POSSESSING KNOWLEDGE OF THESE MATTERS. THEN THEIR MISGUIDED STATEMENTS SPREAD AMONG THE GENERAL PEOPLE AND CIRCULATE AMONG THEM. WE NEED FROM YOU, OUR ESTEEMED SCHOLAR, A CLARIFICATION REGARDING THIS ISSUE, SO BY ALLAAH WHAT IS YOUR VIEW OF THIS?

nswer: It is obligatory that the Muslim be cautious in regard to the affairs of his religion and not take rulings from just any person, regardless of whether this is taken from a written source, from a media broadcast, or any other way, which has not been verified. This is regardless of whether the person is a secularist or not; it is required that you verify whom you take rulings in the religion from. Not everyone who in fact issues rulings is truly of those with the understanding to properly understand rulings. Therefore is it required that you verify what is stated. What is meant by this is that the believer is cautious regarding the affairs of his religion, and does not hastily enter into matters, or take religious rulings from other than those known to be capable to issue them. Rather, verify this such that you stop at what is proper, and ask the scholars who are well known for their uprightness and the merit and high level of their knowledge such that you act cautiously in regard to the affairs of your religion. Allaah, the Most High, said, *Ask the people of knowledge if you do not know* -(Surah an-Nahl: 43), "the people of knowledge" are those people with knowledge of the Book of Allaah and the Sunnah. You do not ask someone who is accused of not being sound and steadfast in his religion, or the one whose knowledge you are not aware of, or the one who is known to have deviated from the methodology of the people of the Sunnah.

[FROM A COLLECTION OF RULINGS AND VARIOUS STATEMENTS': VOL. 6, PAGE 64]

(16)

QUESTION: IT IS COMMONLY SAID AMONG SOME OF THE PEOPLE THAT THE ONE WHO DOES NOT HAVE A SCHOLAR, SHAYTAAN IS HIS SCHOLAR. SO WHAT IS YOUR GUIDANCE FOR THEM, ESTEEMED SHEIKH?

nswer: This is a mistake found from the average person, and is ignorance originating with some of the Sufees in order to encourage the people to attach themselves to them and blindly follow them in their innovations and false matters of misguidance. If an individual gains understanding by attending circles of religious knowledge, or contemplating the Qur'aan and the Sunnah and he benefits from that, then one cannot say his scholar is Shaytaan. Rather we say he has struggled in seeking knowledge and attained significant good.

However, it is necessary for the student of knowledge to attach himself to those scholars who are well-known for having sound beliefs and a good record, in order to ask regarding matters which he has difficulty understanding. If he does not ask the people of knowledge he will make many mistakes and many matters will deceive him. Whereas if he attends gatherings of knowledge and listens to the preaching and teaching of the people of knowledge, then through this he can achieve tremendous good and gather many benefits, even if he does not have a specific scholar he studies with. There is no doubt that the one who attends gatherings of knowledge and listens to the Friday sermon, the sermons on the days of 'eid, and the general lectures that are given in the masjids, has many scholars, even if he has not associated himself to one specific scholar whom he blindly follows and adheres to his opinions.

[FROM 'A COLLECTION OF RULINGS AND VARIOUS STATEMENTS': VOL.6, PAGE 430)]

(17)

GAINING KNOWLEDGE OF GOOD AND EVIL
IS ACHIEVED THROUGH STUDYING

o it is necessary, my Muslim brother, that you gain knowledge of what is good through studying and seeking to understand the religion. Likewise, it is necessary to comprehend evil by this same manner, and then to proceed to fulfill the obligation of enjoining the good and forbidding evil. Certainly, possessing insight and understanding in the religion is from the signs of being granted well-being and happiness, and from the indications that Allaah wants goodness for His worshiper. It is narrated in the two "Saheeh" collections of the Imaam al-Bukhaaree and Imaam Muslim on the authority of Mu'aweeyah, may Allaah be pleased with him, on the Prophet, may Allaah's praise and salutations be upon him, that he said, *{Whoever Allaah intends good for He grants him understanding in the religion.}* [1]. So if you see an individual who sticks closely to the circles of knowledge, and inquires about knowledge and gains understanding and insight in the matters of knowledge, then this is from the signs that Allaah intends good for him. He should hold fast to this way, and continue to strive, neither being diverted nor weakening in his effort. As the Prophet, upon him be Allaah's praise and salutations, stated in an authentic narration, *{The one who takes the path of seeking knowledge, Allaah makes easy for him the path to Jannah.}* [2].

---

[1] Narrated in Saheeh al-Bukhaaree: 71, 3116, 7312/ Saheeh Muslim: 1037/ Sunan Ibn Maajah: 221/ al-Muwatta Maalik: 1300, 1667/Musnad Imaam Ahmad: 16395: 16404, and other than these two/ Musannaf Ibn Abee Shaybah:31792/ Sunan ad-Daaramee: 224, 226/- on the authority of Mu'aweeyah, and it is found in Jaame'a al-Tirmidhee: 2645/ Musnad Imaam Ahmad: 2786 /Sunan ad-Daaramee: 270, 2706/- on the authority of Ibn 'Abbaas, and it is found in Sunan Ibn Maajah:220/ Musannaf 'Abdul-Razzaaq: 30851/- on the authority of Abu Hurairah. It was declared authentic by Sheikh al-Albaanee in Saheeh al-Aadab al-Mufrad: 517, Silsilat al-Hadeeth as-Saheehah: 1194, 1195, 1196, Saheeh at-Targheeb at-Tarheeb: 67, as well as in other of his books. Sheikh Muqbil declared it authentic in al-Jaame'a al-Saheeh: 9, 3123, 4650, may Allaah have mercy upon them both.
[2] Narrated in Saheeh Muslim: 2699/ Sunan at-Tirmidhee: 2945/ Sunan Ibn Maajah: 225 / & Musnad Ahmad: 7379- from the hadeeth of Abu Hurairah. Declared authentic by Sheikh al-Albaanee in Saheeh at-Targheeb wa al-Tarheeb: 69, 89, as well as in other of his books.

So seeking knowledge has a tremendous position, and is from jihaad in the path of Allaah, and is from the causes of success, and is from the signs that one is upon goodness. This may be through attending sittings and circles of knowledge, or through reading and studying beneficial books if you are from those who can understand their content. It may be through listening to sermons and beneficial reminders, or through putting questions to the people of knowledge. All of these are beneficial means and paths. Also, it may be accomplished by memorizing the noble Qur'aan, as it is the foundation of knowledge. The noble Qur'aan is the head of every form of knowledge, it is a tremendous foundation, and it is the firm and solid rope of Allaah. It is the greatest book and the most noble of books and it is the most tremendous foundation leading to goodness, and the most significant barrier against evil reaching you.

[FROM "THE OBLIGATION OF ENJOINING THE GOOD AND FORBIDDING EVIL": PAGE 22-27]

(18)

QUESTION: I AM A STUDENT IN AN INSTITUTE. I AM TWENTY ONE YEARS OLD, AND FROM THE BLESSINGS OF ALLAAH UPON ME ARE FAITH IN ALLAAH AND THE DECISION TO REJECT THAT WHICH I PREVIOUSLY HELD, AND I HAVE ABANDONED THESE AFFAIRS AND I ASK ALLAAH'S FORGIVENESS. WHAT IS THE BEST PATH FOR ME TO BE GUIDED TO? MAY ALLAAH BLESS YOU WITH GOOD.

nswer: I direct and encourage you towards firmly holding to repentance from the previous errors you engaged in, that you sincerely regret them, that you stand firmly upon the obedience of Allaah and His Messenger, and that you have a sincere resolve to not return to that sin and wrongdoing. I also advise you to frequently read the Book of Allaah, and to carefully consider its meanings, and that you frequently struggle to memorize collections of the hadeeth narrations of the Prophet such as *((Bulugh al-Maraam)02-34)* by Haafidh Ibn Hajr *(('Amdatul-Hadeeth)02-29)* by Haafidh 'Abdul-Ghanee al-Maqdasee *(('Arba'een an-Nawawee)02-27)* and that work which adds other narrations completing those forty narrations, as well as *((Kitaab at-Tawheed)06-01)* by Sheikh Muhammad Ibn 'Abdul-Wahaab, and *((al-Aqeedatul-Wasateeyah)06-05)* by Sheikh al-Islaam Ibn Taymeeyah, and also *((Kashf ash-Shubahaat)06-04)* by Sheikh Muhammad Ibn 'Abdul-Wahaab. We also advise you to review and refer to the book *((Zaad al-Ma'ad Fee Haadee Khair al-Ebaad)09-05)* by Ibn Qayyim, as it is a book of tremendous benefit. Similarly benefit from the work *((Fath al-Majeed Sharh Kitaab at-Tawheed)06-12)* by Sheikh 'Abdur-Rahman Ibn Hasan

[FROM 'COLLECTION OF RULINGS AND VARIOUS STATEMENTS': VOL. 9, PAGE 362]

(19)

EXPLANATION OF SOME OF THE MATTERS
AND BOOKS WHICH ARE IMPORTANT FOR
CALLING TO ALLAAH.

From 'Abdul-'Azeez Ibn 'Abdullah Ibn Baaz, to our esteemed noble brother, may Allaah grant him success.

Assalaamu 'aleikum wa rahmatAllaah wa barakatuhu.

As for what follows:

Indeed we received your letter in which you acknowledged the benefit you gained from the books which were sent to you by the head of the Islamic affairs ministry, as well as your inquiries regarding some of the affairs which are essential to the effort of calling to Allaah.

Indeed you should know that it is obligatory upon the one who calls to Allaah to have insight and understanding of that which he is inviting to, and that he contemplate and consider the meanings of what is contained in the Qur'aan, the Sunnah, and the statements of the people of knowledge in relation to what every matter he intends to speak about. If one's speech is regarding the obligation to worship Allaah alone and to abandon associating anything or anyone with him, then he should consider and reflect upon those hadeeth narrations related to this issue; and refer back to the explanations and statements of the people of knowledge such as in *((Tafseer Ibn Katheer)01-01)*, *((Tafseer Ibn Jareer)01-04)*, and *((Tafseer Ibn Baghawee)01-07)*, until he achieves clarity in his understanding of the right of Allaah to be worshiped alone, and in his understanding the reality of associating others with Him in worship.

From the best specific books in this subject are the books of Sheikh al-Islaam Ibn Taymeeyah, Ibn Qayyim, and Sheikh Muhammad Ibn 'Abdul-Wahaab, as well as those who follow the methodology they proceeded upon from the other people of knowledge. From the beneficial books in this subject are *((Zaad al-Ma'ad Fee Haadee Khair al-Ebaad)09-05)* by Ibn Qayyim, and *((al-Qa'edah al-Jaleelah Fee at-Tawassul wa al-Waseelah)06-49)* Sheikh al-Islaam Ibn Taymeeyah, as well as his work *((al-Aqeedatul-Wasateeyah)06-05)*.

Also there is *((Kitaab at-Tawheed)06-01)* by Sheikh Muhammad Ibn 'Abdul-Wahaab and *((Fath al-Majeed)06-12)* by his grandson Sheikh 'Abdur-Rahman Ibn Hasan.

And if his speech will be regarding ritual prayer, obligatory charity, or issues other than these from among the secondary matters, then one should work with those source texts which are relevant to that issue, and guide the one he is calling to that issue which he are teaching him by summarizing matters, having excellent behavior, and using comprehensive expressions in order to facilitate the attaining an understanding by the one he is calling and inviting. As for that which is related to translation, then it is possible for the student of knowledge to rely upon the one that he knows has sound beliefs and possesses knowledge along with an understanding of that foreign language into which he wishes to translate the desired statement. He should utilize some of the Islamic books which are in English and French languages along with volumes one and two of our book *(Collection of Rulings and Various Statements)07-17)*.

I ask Allaah, the Most Perfect, to guide all of us together to the right path, and that He gives success to you and to us in being directed to that which He loves and is pleased with. Indeed He is the one who hears and is close.

Assalaamu 'aleikum wa rahmatAllaahi wa barakatuhu.

[FROM 'A COLLECTION OF RULINGS AND VARIOUS STATEMENTS': VOL. 5, PAGE 428]

(20)

UNITY, ADHERENCE TO THE RELIGION, AND THEIR REQUIREMENTS: IN DISCUSSING WHAT WAS WRITTEN BY SOMEONE, IT WAS MENTIONED TO SHEIKH IBN BAAZ THAT IN HIS FOURTH ARTICLE THIS PERSON CALLED TO GIVING PRIORITY TO ATTAINING UNITY BETWEEN THE DIFFERENT MUSLIM GROUPS AND IN COOPERATION UPON JIHAD AGAINST THE ENEMIES OF ISLAM. HE ALSO MENTIONED THAT THIS IS NOT THE TIME TO CRITICIZE THOSE WHO ADHERE TO A SPECIFIC SCHOOL OF FIQH WITH BIGOTRY, OR THE SECT OF THE 'ASHAREES, OR THE GROUP KNOWN AS "THE MUSLIM BROTHERHOOD," OR EVEN THE FOLLOWERS OF SUFISM.

In response he said: There is no doubt that it is an obligation upon the Muslims to unify their ranks and unite their voices as one upon the truth, and to cooperate among themselves in goodness and fearing Allaah against the enemies of Islaam, as Allaah, the Most Perfect has commanded them in His, the Most High and the Most Exalted, statement, *And hold fast, all of you together, to the Rope of Allaah, and be not divided among yourselves*-(Surah Aal-'Imraan:103). He warned them against separating and division in His statement, *And be not as those who divided and differed among themselves after the clear proofs had come to them*-(Surah Aal-'Imraan:105).However, the obligation to unite the Muslims and join their voices together upon the truth, and to hold fast to the rope of Allaah, does not require the abandoning of forbidding wrongdoing whether from actions or beliefs of the followers of Sufism or others. Rather, doing so is itself a requirement of the command to hold fast to the rope of Allaah and to enjoin good and forbid wrongdoing, and to make clear the truth for the one who has strayed from it, or who believes something which opposes the truth with evidences from the Sharee'ah until we are united upon the truth and have rejected that which opposes it. This is a requirement of the statement of Allaah, *Help you one another in goodness and piety but do not help one another in sin and transgression.*-(Surah al-Maidah:2) and the statement of Allaah, the Most Perfect : *Let there arise out of you a group of people inviting to all that is good (Islaam), enjoining every matter of good and forbidding every matter of wrongdoing and evil. And it is they who are the successful.*-(Surah Aal-'Imraan:104).

When the people of truth are silent and refrain from explaining mistakes of those who have made them, and the errors of those who have fallen into them, then they have not fulfilled that which Allaah has commanded them from calling to good and enjoining what is right and forbidding wrongdoing. Furthermore, it is well known what results from this sin of refraining from forbidding evil; it is that the one who is in error remains in error, and the one who has opposed the truth stays upon his mistake. This contradicts what Allaah has legislated from giving advice and cooperation upon good and enjoining what is right and forbidding what is wrong. And Allaah is our guardian and the giver of success.

['A COLLECTION OF RULINGS AND VARIOUS STATEMENTS': VOL. 3, PAGE 68.]

(21)

QUESTION: PLEASE GUIDE ME TO THE WAY THAT WILL ASSIST ME IN MEMORIZING THE BOOK OF ALLAAH

nswer: I advise you to concentrate and be committed to this matter and to select the most suitable times for memorization, such as the later part of the night or after Fajr prayer or sometime during the night, or at the other times when you can feel comfortable, such that you can memorize well. Also I advise you to choose a good companion who will help and assist you in your memorization and study. Along with this, seek success and assistance in this endeavor from Allaah and humbly ask Him to help you, grant you success, and to guide you to the means of success. As the one who sincerely seeks assistance from Allaah, then Allaah will support him and facilitate his efforts.

[FROM 'A COLLECTION OF RULINGS AND VARIOUS STATEMENTS:' VOL. 6, PAGE 374]

(22)

QUESTION: WHAT IS THE RULING OF THE ONE WHO RECITES QUR'AAN BUT MAKES MISTAKES IN THE PRONUNCIATION OF SHORT VOWELS? WILL HE BE REWARDED FOR SUCH A RECITATION?

nswer: It has been legislated that the believer strive to recite properly, and work to assess what is correct in his effort. He should recite to someone who is more knowledgeable than him in the knowledge of reciting Qur'aan until he benefits and is able to correct the mistakes he has. He is rewarded and he is indeed given two rewards if he struggles in reciting and works to correct his mistakes, as is seen in the statement of the Prophet, may Allaah's praise and salutations be upon him, *{The proficient reciter of the Qur'aan is associated with the noble and the upright, recording angels, and the one who makes mistakes and finds it difficult for him will have a double reward}* [1]. This is the wording of the narration as found in Saheeh Muslim.

[FROM 'A COLLECTION OF RULINGS AND VARIOUS STATEMENTS': VOL. 9, PAGE 416]

[1]

(23)

QUESTION: I HAVE OFTEN MEMORIZED VERSES OF THE NOBLE QUR'AAN; HOWEVER AFTER SOME TIME PASSES I FORGET WHAT I MEMORIZED. SIMILARLY, WHEN I RECITE I AM NOT SURE WHETHER MY RECITATION IS CORRECT OR NOT. AFTERWARD I DISCOVER THAT I INDEED MADE MISTAKES IN MY RECITATION. SO KINDLY OFFER ME GUIDANCE REGARDING THIS.

nswer: The Sharee'ah guidance for you my brother is that you put forth your effort to memorize that which is easy for you from the Book of Allaah, and that you read back and review what you've memorized to some of your good brothers at school, in the masjid, or in your home. Additionally you should be diligent in this until your recitation is correct and sound. This is due to the statement of the Prophet, may Allaah's praise and salutations be upon him, *{The best of you are those who learn the Qur'aan and teach it.}* [1], as was narrated by al-Bukhaaree in his "Saheeh" collection of hadeeth narrations. Therefore the best people are those who are attached to the Qur'aan and have learned it, and then taught it to the people, and acted upon it, implementing its guidance. This is due to the statement of the Prophet, may Allaah's praise and salutations be upon him, *{"Which of you would like to go out every morning to Buthan and bring two large she–camels without being guilty of sin or without achieving it by severing the ties of kinship?" We said: "Messenger of Allah, all of us would like to do it." Upon this he said: "Does not one of you go out in the morning to the mosque and teach or recite two verses from the Book of Allah. the Majestic and Glorious? That is better for him than two she–camels, and three verses are better than three she–camels, and four verses are better for him than four she–camels, and so on in their number in camels."}* [2] or as the Messenger of Allaah, may Allaah's praise and salutations be upon him, has stated.

This makes clear to us the high merit of teaching the Qur'aan. So it is upon you my brother to learn the Qur'aan from those brothers who are knowledgeable of its proper recitation, until you benefit from this and are able to recite correctly.

[1]   Narrated in Saheeh al-Bukhaaree: 5027/ Sunan Abee Dawud: 1352/Sunan at-Tirmidhee: 2907/ & Musnad Ahmad: 414, 502/ from the hadeeth of 'Uthmaan Ibn 'Afaan. Declared authentic by Sheikh al-Albaanee in Silsilatul-Hadeeth Saheehah: 1173, and in Saheeh at-Targheeb wa at-Tarheeb: 1415, as well as in other of his works.

[2]   Narrated in Sunan Abu Dawud: 1257/ -on the authority of 'Uqbah Ibn 'Aamr. It was declared authentic by Sheikh al-Albaanee in al-Albaanee in Silsilat al-Hadeeth as-Saheehah: 1456 and within other of his works.

As for that which you've encountered of forgetfulness, then there is no blame upon you for this. Everyone forgets some matters. Just as Prophet, may Allaah's praise and salutations be upon his said, *{Indeed I'm a human being like you, and I forget as you forget.}* And once he was reciting and someone corrected him, and he said, *{May Allaah have mercy upon so and so, he reminded me of the verse which I missed or did not recall.}* -(Saheeh Muslim: 1353) What is intended by this is that an individual may forget certain verses and then later remember them, or someone else will remind him of what is correct regarding them. So what is better is that you say "I was made to forget." or "I was caused to forget.". This is due to what is narrated that the Prophet said "one of you should not saying I forgot that verse, rather he was made to forget by Shaytaan."

As for that hadeeth narration which says [The one who memorizes the Qur'aan and then forgets it, will meet Allaah in a state in which he is mutilated.], then this narration is weak and not authentically affirmed as a saying from the Prophet. Forgetfulness is not something which one chooses or which one has the capacity to preserve himself from. So again what is intended according to the guidance of the Sharee'ah is that you memorize that which is easy for you from the Book of Allaah, the Most Glorified and the Most Exalted, and that you maintain and preserve that, as well as reciting what you memorize to one who has good recitation in order to correct your mistakes. And I ask Allaah to grant you success in this affair of yours.

[FROM 'A COLLECTION OF RULINGS AND VARIOUS STATEMENTS': VOL.6, PAGE 373]

THE NAKHLAH
EDUCATIONAL SERIES:

The Purpose of the 'Nakhlah Educational Series' is to contribute to the present knowledge based efforts which enable Muslim individuals, families, and communities to understand and learn Islaam and then to develop within and truly live Islaam. Our commitment and goal is to contribute beneficial publications and works that:

Firstly, reflect the priority, message and methodology of all the prophets and messengers sent to humanity, meaning that single revealed message which embodies the very purpose of life, and of human creation. As Allaah the Most High has said,

❁ *We sent a Messenger to every nation ordering them that they should worship Allaah alone, obey Him and make their worship purely for Him, and that they should avoid everything worshipped besides Allaah. So from them there were those whom Allaah guided to His religion, and there were those who were unbelievers for whom misguidance was ordained. So travel through the land and see the destruction that befell those who denied the Messengers and disbelieved.*❁ –(Surah an-Nahl: 36)

Secondly, building upon the above foundation, our commitment is to contributing publications and works which reflect the inherited message and methodology of the acknowledged scholars of the many various branches of Sharee'ah knowledge who stood upon the straight path of preserved guidance in every century and time since the time of our Messenger, may Allaah's praise and salutations be upon him. These people of knowledge, who are the inheritors of the Final Messenger, have always adhered closely to the two revealed sources of guidance: the Book of Allaah and the Sunnah of the Messenger of Allaah- may Allaah's praise and salutations be upon him, upon the united consensus, standing with the body of guided Muslims in every century - preserving and transmitting the true religion generation after generation. Indeed the Messenger of Allaah, may Allaah's praise and salutations be upon him, informed us that, *{ A group of people amongst my Ummah will remain obedient to Allaah's orders. They will not be harmed by those who leave them nor by those who oppose them, until Allaah's command for the Last Day comes upon them while they remain on the right path. }* (Authentically narrated in Saheeh al-Bukhaaree).

The guiding scholar Sheikh Zayd al-Madkhalee, may Allaah protect him, stated in his writing, 'The Well Established Principles of the Way of the First Generations of Muslims: It's Enduring & Excellent Distinct Characteristics' that,

"From among these principles and characteristics is that the methodology of tasfeeyah -or clarification, and tarbeeyah -or education and cultivation- is clearly affirmed and established as a true way coming from the first three generations of Islaam, and is something well known to the people of true merit from among them, as is concluded by considering all the related evidence.

What is intended by tasfeeyah, when referring to it generally, is clarifying that which is the truth from that which is falsehood, what is goodness from that which is harmful and corrupt, and when referring to its specific meanings it is distinguishing the noble Sunnah of the Prophet and the people of the Sunnah from those innovated matters brought into the religion and the people who are supporters of such innovations.

As for what is intended by tarbeeyah, it is calling all of the creation to take on the manners and embrace the excellent character invited to by that guidance revealed to them by their Lord through His worshiper and Messenger Muhammad, may Allaah's praise and salutations be upon him; so that they might have good character, manners, and behavior. As without this they cannot have a good life, nor can they put right their present condition or their final destination. And we seek refuge in Allaah from the evil of not being able to achieve that rectification."

Thus the methodology of the people of standing upon the Prophet's Sunnah, and proceeding upon the 'way of the believers' in every century is reflected in a focus and concern with these two essential matters: tasfeeyah or clarification of what is original, revealed message from the Lord of all the worlds, and tarbeeyah or education and raising of ourselves, our families, and our communities, and our lands upon what has been distinguished to be that true message and path.

METHODOLOGY:

The Roles of the Scholars & General Muslims In Raising the New Generation

The priority and focus of the 'Nakhlah Educational Series' is reflected within in the following statements of Sheikh al-Albaanee, may Allaah have mercy upon him:

"As for the other obligation, then I intend by this the education of the young generation upon Islaam purified from all of those impurities we have mentioned, giving them a correct Islamic education from their very earliest years, without any influence of a foreign, disbelieving education."

(Silsilat al-Hadeeth ad-Da'eefah, Introduction page 2.)

"...And since the Messenger of Allaah, may Allaah's praise and salutations be upon him, has indicated that the only cure to remove this state of humiliation that we find ourselves entrenched within, is truly returning back to the religion. Then it is clearly obligatory upon us - through the people of knowledge- to correctly and properly understand the religion in a way that conforms to the sources of the Book of Allaah and the Sunnah, and that we educate and raise a new virtuous, righteous generation upon this."

(Clarification and Cultivation and the Need of the Muslims for Them)

It is essential in discussing our perspective upon this obligation of raising the new generation of Muslims, that we highlight and bring attention to a required pillar of these efforts as indicated by Sheikh al-Albaanee, may Allaah have mercy upon him, and others- in the golden words, *"through the people of knowledge"*. Since something we commonly experience today is that many people have various incorrect understandings of the role that the scholars should have in the life of a Muslim, failing to understand the way in which they fulfill their position as the inheritors of the Messenger of Allaah, may Allaah's praise and salutations be upon him, and stand as those who preserve and enable us to practice the guidance of Islaam.   Similarly the guiding scholar Sheikh 'Abdul-'Azeez Ibn Baaz, may Allaah have mercy upon him, also emphasized this same overall responsibility:

*"...It is also upon a Muslim that he struggles diligently in that which will place his worldly affairs in a good state, just as he must also strive in the correcting of his religious affairs and the affairs of his own family. As the people of his household have a significant right over him that he strive diligently in rectifying their affair and guiding them towards goodness, due to the statement of Allaah, the Most Exalted, ❁ **Oh you who believe! Save yourselves and your families Hellfire whose fuel is men and stones** ❁ -(Surah at-Tahreem: 6)*

*So it is upon you to strive to correct the affairs of the members of your family. This includes your wife, your children- both male and female- and such as your own brothers. This concerns all of the people in your family, meaning you should strive to teach them the religion, guiding and directing them, and warning them from those matters Allaah has prohibited for us. Because you are the one who is responsible for them as shown in the statement of the Prophet, may Allaah's praise and salutations be upon him, { **Every one of you is a guardian, and responsible for what is in his custody. The ruler is a guardian of his subjects*** *and responsible for them; a husband is a guardian of his family and is responsible for it; a lady is a guardian of her husband's house and is responsible for it, and a servant is a guardian of his master's property and is responsible for it....}* Then the Messenger of Allaah, may Allaah's praise and salutations be upon him, continued to say, *{...so all of you are guardians and are responsible for those under your authority.}* *(Authentically narrated in Saheeh al-Bukhaaree & Muslim)*

It is upon us to strive diligently in correcting the affairs of the members of our families, from the aspect of purifying their sincerity of intention for Allaah's sake alone in all of their deeds, and ensuring that they truthfully believe in and follow the Messenger of Allaah, may Allaah's praise and salutations be upon him, their fulfilling the prayer and the other obligations which Allaah the Most Exalted has commanded for us, as well as from the direction of distancing them from everything which Allaah has prohibited.

It is upon every single man and women to give advice to their families about the fulfillment of what is obligatory upon them. Certainly, it is upon the woman as well as upon the man to perform this. In this way our homes become corrected and rectified in regard to the most important and essential matters. Allaah said to His Prophet, may Allaah's praise and salutations be upon him, ﴾ **And enjoin the ritual prayers on your family...** ﴿ *(Surah Taha: 132) Similarly, Allaah the Most Exalted said to His prophet Ismaa'aeel,* ﴾ **And mention in the Book, Ismaa'aeel. Verily, he was true to what he promised, and he was a Messenger, and a Prophet. And he used to enjoin on his family and his people the ritual prayers and the obligatory charity, and his Lord was pleased with him.** ﴿ *-(Surah Maryam: 54-55)*

As such, it is only proper that we model ourselves after the prophets and the best of people, and be concerned with the state of the members of our households. Do not be neglectful of them, oh worshipper of Allaah! Regardless of whether it is concerning your wife, your mother, father, grandfather, grandmother, your brothers, or your children; it is upon you to strive diligently in correcting their state and condition..."

(Collection of Various Rulings and Statements- Sheikh 'Abdul-'Azeez Ibn 'Abdullah Ibn Baaz, Vol. 6, page 47)

We hope to contribute works which enable every striving Muslim who acknowledges the proper position of the scholars, to fulfill the recognized duty and obligation which lays upon each one of us to bring the light of Islaam into our own lives as individuals as well as into our homes and among our families. Towards this goal we are committed to developing educational publications and comprehensive educational curriculums -through cooperation with and based upon the works of the scholars of Islaam and the students of knowledge. Works which, with the assistance of Allaah, the Most High, we can utilize to educate and instruct ourselves, our families and our communities upon Islaam in both principle and practice. The publications and works of the Nakhlah Educational Series are divided into the following categories:

Basic: Ages 4- 6

Elementary: Ages 6-11

Secondary: Ages 11-14

High School: Ages 14- Young Adult

General: Young Adult –Adult

Supplementary: All Ages

Publications and works within these stated levels will, with the permission of Allaah, encompass different beneficial areas and subjects, and will be offered in every permissible form of media and medium. As certainly, as the guiding scholar Sheikh Saaleh Fauzaan al-Fauzaan, may Allaah preserve him, has stated,

"Beneficial knowledge is itself divided into two categories. Firstly is that knowledge which is tremendous in its benefit, as it benefits in this world and continues to benefit in the Hereafter. This is religious Sharee'ah knowledge. And secondly, that which is limited and restricted to matters related to the life of this world, such as learning the processes of manufacturing various goods. This is a category of knowledge related specifically to worldly affairs.

…As for the learning of worldly knowledge, such as knowledge of manufacturing, then it is legislated upon us collectively to learn whatever the Muslims have a need for. Yet If they do not have a need for this knowledge, then learning it is a neutral matter upon the condition that it does not compete with or displace any areas of Sharee'ah knowledge…"

("Explanations of the Mistakes of Some Writers'", Pages 10-12)

We ask Allaah, the most High to bless us with success in contributing to the many efforts of our Muslim brothers and sisters committed to raising themselves as individuals and the next generation of our children upon that Islaam which Allaah has perfected and chosen for us, and which He has enabled the guided Muslims to proceed upon in each and every century. We ask him to forgive us, and forgive the Muslim men and the Muslim women, and to guide all the believers to everything He loves and is pleased with. The success is from Allaah, The Most High The Most Exalted, alone and all praise is due to Him.

Abu Sukhailah Khalil Ibn-Abelahyi
Taalib al-Ilm Educational Resources

BOOK PUBLICATION PREVIEW:

Al-Waajibaat:
The Obligatory Matters

What it is Decreed that Every Male and Female Muslim Must Have Knowledge Of -from the statements of Sheikh al-Islaam Muhammad ibn 'Abdul-Wahaab

(A Step By Step Course on The Fundamental Beliefs of Islaam- with Lesson Questions, Quizzes, & Exams)

*Collected and Arranged by
Umm Mujaahid Khadijah Bint Lacina
al-Amreekiyyah*

[Available: **Now - Self Study/ Teachers Edition**
price: (Soft cover) **$20** (Hard cover) **$27**
Directed Study Edition price: **$17.50** -
Exercise Workbook price: **$10** ¦ eBook **$9.99**]

SCAN WITH SMARTPHONE

FOR MORE INFORMATION

SCAN WITH SMARTPHONE

FOR MORE INFORMATION

BOOK PUBLICATION PREVIEW:

Thalaathatul-Usool: The Three Fundamental Principles

A Step by Step Educational Course on Islaam
Based upon Commentaries of 'Thalaathatul-Usool'
of Sheikh Muhammad ibn 'Abdul Wahaab
(may Allaah have mercy upon him)

*Collected and Arranged by Umm Mujaahid
Khadijah Bint Lacina al-Amreekiyyah*

Description:
*A complete course for the Believing men and women
who want to learn their religion from the ground
up, building a firm foundation upon which to base
their actions. This is the* **second** *in our* **Foundation
Series** *on Islamic beliefs and making them a reality
in your life, which began with* **"al-Waajibaat: The
Obligatory Matters"**.

[Available: **Now Self Study/ Teachers Edition** ¦
price: (Soft cover) **$27.50** (Hard cover) **$35**
Directed Study Edition price: (S) **$22.50** -
Exercise Workbook price: (S) **$12** ¦ eBook **$9.99**]

SCAN WITH SMARTPHONE

FOR MORE INFORMATION

SCAN WITH SMARTPHONE

FOR MORE INFORMATION

BOOK PUBLICATION PREVIEW:

My Hijaab, My Path

A Comprehensive Knowledge Based Compilation on Muslim Women's Role & Dress

Collected and Translated by
Umm Mujaahid Khadijah Bint Lacina
al-Amreekiyyah

[Available: **Now** ¦ pages: **190+** ¦ price: (S) **$17.50**
(H) **$25** ¦ eBook **$9.99**

SCAN WITH SMARTPHONE

FOR MORE INFORMATION

SCAN WITH SMARTPHONE

FOR MORE INFORMATION

BOOK PUBLICATION PREVIEW:

My Home, My Path

A Comprehensive Source Book For Today's Muslim Woman Discussing Her Essential Role & Contribution To The Establishment of Islaam – Taken From The Words Of The People Of Knowledge

Collected and Translated by
Umm Mujaahid Khadijah Bint Lacina
al-Amreekiyyah

[Available: **Now**¦ pages: **420+** ¦ price: (Soft cover) **$25**
(Hard cover) **$35** (eBook) **$9.99**]

SCAN WITH SMARTPHONE

IPRINT

FOR MORE INFORMATION

SCAN WITH SMARTPHONE

EBOOK

FOR MORE INFORMATION

BOOK PUBLICATION PREVIEW:

Fasting from Alif to Yaa:
A Day by Day Guide to Making the Most of Ramadhaan

-Contains additional points of benefit to teach one how to live Islaam as a way of life
-Plus, stories of the Prophets and Messengers including activities for the whole family to enjoy and benefit from for each day of Ramadhaan. Some of the Prophets and Messengers covered include Aadam, Ibraaheem, Lut, Yusuf, Sulaymaan, Shu'ayb, Moosa, Zakariyyah, Muhammad, and more!
-Recipes for foods enjoyed by Muslims around the world

By Umm Mujaahid Khadijah Bint Lacina al-Amreekiyyah as-Salafiyyah With Abu Hamzah Hudhaifah Ibn Khalil and Umm Usaamah Sukhailah Bint Khalil

[Available: **1433** -pages: 250+ | price: (S) **$20** (H) **$27** | eBook **$9.99**

SCAN WITH SMARTPHONE

FOR MORE INFORMATION

SCAN WITH SMARTPHONE

FOR MORE INFORMATION

BOOK PUBLICATION PREVIEW:

The Cure, The Explanation, The Clear Affair, & The Brilliantly Distinct Signpost

A Step by Step Educational Course on Islaam Based upon Commentaries of

'Usul as-Sunnah' of Imaam Ahmad
(may Allaah have mercy upon him)

Study of text divided into chapters formatted into multiple short lessons to facilitate learning . Each lesson has: evidence summary, lesson benefits, standard & review exercises 'Usul as-Sunnah' Arabic text & translation divided for easier memorization.

Compiled and Translated by:
Abu Sukhailah Khalil Ibn-Abelahyi

[Available: **TBA** ¦ price: **TBA** (Multi-volume) ¦ soft cover, hard cover, ebook]

SCAN WITH SMARTPHONE

PRINT

FOR MORE INFORMATION

SCAN WITH SMARTPHONE

EBOOK

FOR MORE INFORMATION

BOOK PUBLICATION PREVIEW:

Whispers of Paradise (1): A Muslim Woman's Life Journal

An Islamic Daily Journal Which Encourages Reflection & Rectification

Collected and Edited by Taalib al-Ilm Educational Resources Development Staff

[Available: **Now** ¦ price: (Soft cover) **$25**]

[New elegantly designed edition is for the year 1438 / 2017]

12 Monthly calendar pages with beneficial quotations from Ibn Qayyim
Daily journal page based upon Islamic calendar (with corresponding C.E. dates)

SCAN WITH SMARTPHONE

FOR MORE INFORMATION